HOW TO WRITE & SELL YOUR FIRST BOOK

How to Write & Sell Your First Book

Don Aslett

Illustrated by Craig LaGory

MARSH CREEK PRESS

How to Write & Sell Your First Book

Published by Marsh Creek Press,
PO Box 700 Pocatello, Idaho 83204
1-888-748-3535; fax 1-208-235-5481.

ISBN 0-937750-29-8

Library of Congress Cataloging-in-Publication Data

Aslett, Don, 1935-
     How to write & sell your first book / Don Aslett ; illustrated by Craig LaGory.
          p. cm.
          ISBN 0-937750-29-8 (hc.)
           1. Authorship. 2. Authorship—Marketing. I. Title: How to write and sell your first book. II. Title.

     PN147 .A7244 2002
     808'.02—dc21   2002141426

Illustrator and designer: Craig LaGory
Editor: Carol Cartaino
Production manager: Tobi Flynn

To Mother (Opal),
who wrote her first book at eighty!

Acknowledgments

Every book we write might carry our byline, but it is a composite of many processes, places, and people. My many successful books have been blessed by my relationship with others, including my editor (and writing partner now for more than twenty years) Carol Cartaino, great artists like Judith Holmes Clarke and Craig LaGory, my right hand (and manager of Marsh Creek Press) Tobi Flynn, the fellow authors who have generously shared their thoughts with me, and my family, friends, and many loyal and helpful employees.

TABLE OF CONTENTS

A seasoned pro with thirty-three books already in print and at least as many in the works, Don Aslett looks at writing as a moral obligation. "We all need to do whatever we can to inspire others and help them live better," he says, "and writing is one of the best ways to do that. We all have a book or two inside us (maybe more) that can benefit others, as well as giving us great pleasure ourselves. I believe that we all can—and should—write that book."

Don has written essays, poems, and articles all his life. He published his first book at the age of forty-five and plans to publish his last at ninety-five. His books (many of them bestsellers) have been published by leading national publishers, translated into many other languages, and offered by numerous book clubs. Don travels constantly to promote his books and appears frequently on radio and TV. He owns and operates several successful businesses, including Varsity Contractors, one of the country's top professional cleaning and maintenance companies, and Marsh Creek Press, his own private publishing company.

Don and his wife, Barbara, have six children and eighteen grandchildren and divide their time between a ranch in southern Idaho and their winter home in Kauai, Hawaii.

A book?
Yours?
Uncomplicate the process!

Writing a book is, in principle, exactly like starting a little business baking brownies or packing for a long vacation. There are no mysteries, not one part of it you can't figure out or do. Your desire to do it will easily override all of the "I don't knows" and "I've never done this befores." There are more than 50,000 books published every year, most of them by people not half as smart as you and who probably don't have nearly as much to say as you have.

When it comes to making a book, remember that there are a few boundaries but no hard and fast rules. People have written entire books on some of the details of book writing, producing, and marketing, and there are writers who have never cracked those books and still come up with a bestseller.

If you can't figure something out from your wits and my information here or the other sources I've suggested, then go to a bookstore and check out what others have done, or invent something that just works and feels good to you. I'm telling you not to get lost in the trivia of detail. Creativity and good ideas (your own fresh ones) will go a long way toward making a readable and salable end product. So read the rules and note the boundaries, but don't get intimidated into being so "correct" that you forget to be an enthusiastic message bearer who has a passion about something worthwhile. Good books do need many of the ingredients we will discuss in these pages, but a lot of this will evolve naturally once you get into the process. Some things will come by themselves, and some you'll have to think or dig a bit for, but the treasure is there... FOR SURE. And your brain and pen or keyboard are the only tools you really need.

Note: There are some solid principles of book writing and selling that you **must** be aware of and remember, so I will bring up these bits of wisdom in more than one place. The editor was not asleep at the switch—I just wanted to be sure I made you a believer!

CHAPTER I

A BOOK!
YOUR BOOK!!!
(WHY DO IT?)

So you want to write a book. You can!

It's not hard, or complicated.
It doesn't take forever.
It's not expensive.
It's not just for the talented or highly educated.

It's so possible, and so rewarding, if you really want to do it. If there is one nonexclusive undertaking in this universe, it is writing a book. You've read hundreds of them and you already know much of what there is to know about books. A book isn't just for intellectuals or the elite—it's something that any one of us can see, feel, lift, read, use, and own. And write!

If you want to do your own book, you can. You don't have to be a certain age, sex, creed, or color to do one or have extraordinary skills and talents. Doing a book is an entirely possible project that you can start today! There are few rules, no schedule made by anyone else but you, no taskmasters—you are 100 percent in control of it all.

The big downer in book writing comes when you spend all your time and mind getting ready to write instead of writing, or get bogged down in, discouraged, or diverted by all the mechanics of the process.

The usual approach, once someone has decided to write a book, is to seek out and research all the how-to of the process (how others did it, that is)—take a writing class, buy a computer, and somehow bury yourself in preparations, leaving no energy for actual production!

This book you are reading began exactly like your book will. I kept running into people who told me they'd thought about doing a book, and still wanted to. I knew a lot about doing books—I'd done more than thirty successful ones in my spare time. So I made a mental note of all this interest, kept it on a back burner in my mind, and then started collecting thoughts and ideas on it. I knew there were plenty of "how to write a book" books out there somewhere. But that didn't discourage me, nor should competing books discourage you (see chapter three).

If I followed my college professor's advice about writing to do this (by the way, he never published anything), book I would have collected a dozen or so of those other "how to write a book" books, studied them, outlined them, digested them, and then written. I'm not convinced that "research" is the first or the key ingredient of a book that truly lives. We already have too many books that are just conscientious summaries and condensations of other books. That can easily mean a dull and inbred book.

A simple recipe that works

I didn't read one single "how others do it" book or article to do this, even though I know there are some good ones out there. You will get here a new, fresh (yes, even over-opinionated) set of rules for how to write, not a summary of how others or the big ten do it. Let the big ten do their own teaching; that's not my job or talent. I'm coming at you from a practical, down-home direction. I'm going to give you a simple recipe that I know works. It isn't intended to be "the" way to do a book. It is the way a common, average person like me (a farmer and janitor) did it, and does it, every day and week and year.

My credibility doesn't come from a degree, grade point average, or fancy training of any kind. It comes from a solid record of production. I started writing books when I was forty-five and have produced more than thirty good books since then. I have as many or more in the works, on my assembly line. I'm a self-publisher, and I've also had my books published by the biggest and best—Writer's Digest, Betterway Books, Dell, Simon & Schuster, and New American Library. I've sold more than three million books and had many bestsellers. My books have been featured by Book-of-the-Month Club and many other clubs, and been translated into at least nine other languages. I've sold books to publishers, by mail, at my seminars, on TV, and to cleaning product companies and the military. I've done thousands of public appearances and media promotions (TV and radio appearances, newspaper and magazine interviews, and autographings). I've worked with some of the best "book pros" around and I am going to give you some experienced and seasoned advice and a simple, simple procedure for doing YOUR BOOK.

This isn't the only or "THE" way, but the way
a common, average person (a farmer and janitor)
like me did it and does it!

Overestimating can overwhelm you... don't let it

Again, if you check out too many "how to write a book" books and articles from the library, you may end up confused and discouraged. Everyone trying to tell you how to write a book will point out all the "might bes" and "what ifs" and "look outs" there are, all the possible problems or obstacles of the book writing process, many of which you may never encounter. Getting in too deep and too detailed like this is like reading all the books and articles out there on raising children. If you did that, you'd never even consider having a kid. Starting a book is about as much fun, and easy as starting a baby, and handling the ifs, mights, and maybes that come along in the process is not really that tough or that scary. It's not impossible, as hearing all the downsides and horror stories might make you feel.

Writing a book—your book—is not only possible, but overall it will be an easy and pleasant experience if you really want to do it. If it's a casual desire or passing wish or whim, I wouldn't advise you to do it yet. "Want to" is the winner here!

The basic things you need 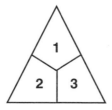 **Something to write about**

 The passion or need to write about it

 The willingness to do it

All the rest will fall into place.

Seven big reasons to write your book

1. It doesn't take that much time.

Some books may be years in the making, but the actual writing time for most books is only a matter of months or even less. I drafted two of my best ones in less than a month during a full, busy schedule of shows and

meetings. For some that took five years to produce, I spent only minutes a week, so in that five years I probably used only about a week of actual time collecting notes, a couple of weeks assembling and writing, and generally another week polishing them up. Sure, months go by, but regular life goes on while you write. I personally never take time off to do nothing but write. I just knit it in with my work, play, and family life.

2. It will build confidence and self-esteem.

The things you fear yourself and admire in others will be changed forever once you do your book. Suddenly something others ("famous people") do, you just did, and probably as well or better. You'll find that fear is gone and some of that admiration you had for others is now yours. It will be quite a boost.

3. It's easier than ever before.

Once we only had rock to write on, and for centuries, too, reproducing what we wrote was painful if not impossible. A mere forty years ago, copies were carbon, typewriters slow, corrections tedious, and typesetting expensive and not accessible to the average person. Now in the day of desktop publishing, computers and word processors are everywhere, and for pennies, in seconds, they can not just typeset but also spellcheck and help organize our writing, lay it out, design it, and print it to perfection. If you don't own a computer, there are millions of computer nuts around who will be flattered to do the job inexpensively or maybe even for free, if you are a good cook or back patter. My beautiful, world-famous books are now done on a $1,500 computer—ready to print. What took weeks or months and thousands of dollars when I started in 1979 takes hours and only hundreds of dollars today. And it is better quality!

4. It will expand and enrich you.

Doing your book beats traveling, vacations, taking more classes, and a lot of socializing. You will encounter interesting new people and places you've never been. Books expose you to new friends, new skills, new knowledge, and new fields, all of which enriches your life. And the process and project of doing your book will teach you much about management and organization. Your book will entertain and edify you more than anything else you've ever done, and even if it doesn't sell one copy or influence one single other life, it will yours. Your book is worth doing for this alone!

5. Your life is already a book.

Haven't we all read the life history of famous people and said to ourselves, "Man, my life is more exciting than that!" Your life is unique—you have ideas, experiences, and thoughts that no one else has. There is little difference between you and "someone famous"— only how many people now know you. Not quality, love, or feelings. You have as much or more in you than many "celebrities," and if you can capture it, your book can be of equal value.

6. Preservation of information/personal history.

Every book we write is an autobiography of some kind, and for our family and the record, we all ought to write our "journal." No matter what your book is about, it is always a personal history in some way. This is of incalculable value to your family alone, as well as the rest of the world. Most books **are** their authors, and your book is a record that will endure long after your passing.

7. You just plain WANT TO.

The biggest reason to write a book is that you've thought about it for a long time, and you just plain want to. To me that is reason enough to go ahead. There are a lot of "want tos" in us, but some we could never pull off, and others we can't afford, or don't have the time or resources for. And some of the things we want to do just aren't nice or right for us or others. But there is one "want to"—your book—that you can do, can afford, and have the time, money, and resources for. And no matter what the outcome, whether your book is good or bad, sells or doesn't sell, you'll gain all kinds of personal value from it and will have satisfied a desire, fulfilled that promise you've made to yourself and others so many times:

"Someday I'm going to write a book."

Everyone has a story to tell. Through the years I've found that to be true. Stop any stranger on the street, and they can tell you any number of stories that will make you laugh, cry, and affect your life.

You are like that, too. You have feelings no one knows about. You want to be heard and listened to, you have lots of thoughts and ideas and opinions, and you want to record some of your stories and experiences too. You may not have put your feelings on paper yet, but you feel the urge to. I am that way, all people are that way, and plenty of us have timidly taken steps to record some of those thoughts and feelings. So go one step further now, and WRITE YOUR BOOK!

Two dozen more GOOD REASONS to write a book

- To express an idea.
- To express yourself. For most people, the need to share an experience or speak out comes before any desire to be famous or make money from an idea.
- To tell a story.
- To feel fulfilled.
- To get something off your chest, or call attention to a cause. One great way to satisfy your causes and concerns, your personal or public irritations, is to write about them. When you see an injustice and think you have an answer for it, write it down!

- To enlighten readers or make them aware of new perspectives.
- To teach readers how to do something.
- To set an example.
- To increase your credibility.
- To make money.
- To travel.
- To get on TV and radio.
- To learn more about a subject.
- To become an expert in a field.
- To get a sense of accomplishment.
- To make someone proud of you.
- To inform and inspire others.
- To start a new hobby.
- To replace some of that "TV time" with something more productive.
- To involve other people in your life. A book can give you a new circle of acquaintances, one based on who you are, not just how cute you are.
- To get speaking opportunities. Your book can put you on a lecture circuit that leads to more money, more fun, and more friends.
- To have new things to talk about to people.
- To learn about the publishing field.
- To make the world a better place to live.

WRITING IS:
Recording inspiration
Changing lives for the better
The best friend you've ever had yet
An independent way to make money

"Why do I write? To hear myself think, to be heard."
—*Patricia Penton Leimbach,*
farm wife and author

A CAUSE—key to success

The very first thing I would do if I were you is identify **the reason you want to write.**

BEFORE you start in on a book venture, make sure you have a real cause and purpose for it. If you are writing for a simple keep-busy sideline or a "maybe hobby" pastime, you are in for a long, probably disappointing experience.

> *If you don't have a good cause or purpose,*
> *DON'T START*

If you are writing just for something to do, on a whim or dare, to show off, or just to see if you can, your book will end up punishing you (and probably others). The fuel to feed a book has to come from deep inside you, and if you just skim the surface, your inspiration and endurance will be about equivalent. Make sure the wound was deep enough, the injustice significant enough, the victory exciting enough, the tale engrossing enough, the pill bitter enough to move you to relive it on the page. If so, it has a chance of affecting many other people, maybe millions.

A cause isn't ax grinding. You aren't writing to "get even," but to be read.

Okay—what is a cause strong enough to coax you away from TV, the table, the golf course, or the kitchen and to keep a pen in your hand and keep you focused for a fortnight and more? Here are some examples:

—You want to share a craft or skill you know well.
—You want to share hope.
—You've had a great loss or gain that others have or could have.
—You have a unique perspective on something.
—You want to save the environment.
—You have a son or daughter you want to leave a heritage for.

A strong enough cause or reason for your book will outdo talent, financing, and luck and override criticism or discouragement. It is the key to beginning your book, so before you launch yourself, lay all worries about outcome aside and cement in your cause, your reason, your motive for your book.

> I am writing this book because I really want to
> _____.*
>
> * some help words for you here:
>
> | | | |
> |---|---|---|
> | share | teach | bless |
> | change | entertain | support |
> | tell | help | uplift |

And by the way, if your main cause or reason is "to get rich," I wouldn't start the book.

True, people can and do make money on books, but your chances of doing so, especially on your first one, are slim. As I mentioned, there are more than 50,000 new books every year, and I'll bet many authors make less than $5,000 on their book, even many seasoned writers. My first book went on the bestseller list and sold a million, and my second book sold almost half a million. But if we were going to have lunch on the proceeds of one or two of my other books, you'd have to buy!

Now don't be disappointed already. I didn't say you can't or won't make money on your book—you might make a lot. There are first-time authors, including self-published authors, who have made tens or hundreds of thousands on their book over time. I'm saying **don't make profit your main cause or motive** for a book. Money is not a real sustainer, and a good book needs more power than stacks of coins or bills can give it. Later on I'll show you some ways to help your book earn some money. But money usually ends up being a third or fourth-place reward, even for a successful book. What a book does for you always outshines the money aspect—it advances you in your profession, finds you friends, gains you respect if not awe, and forces you out of the narrow little world you may have been living in. Money you'll just spend anyway, and maybe not on something that lasts. But loving and being loved through your book will enhance you and endure, and reward you over and over.

> Writing isn't an instant cash profession, but it can
> be an instant provider of joy and energy.

Writers know they're right!

One last thing I think is key to doing a book is that you've got to not just think but **believe** that you are right. The power to pursue something and finish it comes from you. So you need to be convinced that what you're doing is right and necessary. This book, your book, might be your first real entrepreneurial project. An entrepreneur, as you know, is someone who doesn't like working for others, and is willing to strike out on his own, even at the risk of ridicule or failure. He will start a business, a venture, a project on his own. And what is the prime characteristic of all entrepreneurs? They think they are right. That is where they get their "go power" to risk and wrestle whatever they have to. You will need this to start a book and **see it through.**

CHAPTER 2

What Will It Take to Do a Book, Now?

Just HOW LONG does it take to write a book? Two weeks, two months, two years, or twenty?

The answer is, all of the above.

The first miscalculation most people make when looking at the process from the outside is thinking that one day a big light comes on in your head, you sit down at a computer, and then all those words roll out, the whole story or message. (You might just stop occasionally to rip up a page and toss it on the floor.) But few books of any kind just flow out this way.

One such case for me did come in 1993. I was honored as Idaho Business Leader of the Year and decided to take an idea I had about lessons I learned from the farm and animals and write it up as a book of little parables on how to succeed in business: *Everything I Needed to Know About Business I Learned in the Barnyard*. I had vivid memories of the ranch I grew up on, all of my chores there, my early days in Future Farmers of America and 4-H, and of plantings and harvests and working with my father. I had three easy speaking assignments on my agenda about then with a lot of free "layover" time in the travel involved. In two weeks I wrote the entire book, and it was fun and easy. I didn't have to do any research, ask anyone anything, or get any permissions. And there was no need for complex or detailed instructions in the book. So there was little time, cost, and hassle involved. Just a few long days of memory jogging, several yellow pads and pens, and no TV or breaks for a while.

Other books took eighteen months, or even eighteen years from my enthusiastic first idea until the book was in hand. Some book projects I needed and used help on, and others I did almost entirely myself. When I did the full-size book *Get Organized, Get Published!* with Carol Cartaino (who edits all my books), I wrote on and off a few hours a day from time to time for six months. She took my material, wrote and gathered more, and spent seven hundred hours to hand Writer's Digest a finished manuscript.

The time a book takes depends on

1. How much you know about the subject.

2. How hard you work.

3. How big or complicated the book is.

4. Whether it is illustrated, and how many illustrations there are.

5. How much you have to correspond with, or otherwise deal with, others.

6. How tough or exacting your editor or publisher is (even if it's you).

In my own case, when I divide the number of books I have out (thirty, of all kinds and sizes) into the number of years I've been writing (twenty), this reveals that I do about one and one-third books a year, about eight months per book. I work on about ten books at a time actively and about forty others—books that are on my more long-range lists—more casually. This means there are ten in the actual process of being written daily, and forty more whose files I feed regularly with notes and ideas according to what I run across.

In 1981, for instance, I started a couple of small books for Boy Scouts and other young people called "50 Games You Can Play Without Equipment" and "101 Scrumptious Skits for Groups."

I've thought about, gathered material for, written on, and done art roughs for these for twenty years now, and they still aren't finished. They've just been on the back burners of my priority lists, even though I've invested at least $6,000 worth of labor and art in them. My editor, Carol, on the other hand, worked on "instant books" with the feature writers of The Associated Press that were written and manufactured in one month from start to finish.

The average times involved here if you really hit it:

> six months to write
> one month to edit
> two weeks to rewrite
> one month for art
> two weeks for layout
> six weeks to print

Ten or eleven months should do it!

Just how much does it cost to write a book? $100? $1,000? $10,000?

Again, all of the above. The one big factor here is what *you* are worth, what you charge for your time. If you quit your day job to write your book, then the cost of the writing is significant. If you just write in your spare time, however, the cost of the actual writing will be negligible.

Your own labor aside, it all depends on the outside resources you use—tools, talent, travel, and the like. If you need, for mood or material, to travel to Tahiti and live there for three months, interview thirty people, make a hundred long distance phone calls, explore remote villages and wine, dine, and bribe six natives, you will accumulate some expenses against the book.

The size of your book and the amount of illustrating and editing it needs will all affect the cost. I'm a self-publisher, and not counting my own labor (time), my average cost for a two hundred-page book is:

1. Typing $800

2. Editing $5,500

3. Art (my books are often heavily illustrated; yours may not need as much, or any) *$5,000–$10,000*

4. Final layout $3,000–$4,000 (my books have many illustrations; a type-only book would be much less)

5. Printing (in lots of 10,000) $1.35 a copy

If you publish your book with a publisher, or use one of the less expensive routes to self-publishing, your out-of-pocket expenses will be far less—see chapters eight and ten.

Books are one of the best investments!

When you look at the cost or "investment" of a book, you've got to think of it in terms of its ability to contribute to the whole of your life and others' lives, as well as your pocketbook. Spending money on a book has a couple of angles not everyone considers when they do the arithmetic.

I myself don't count the time I spend writing a book—I write in my spare time, for the love of it, and for recreation. Basically, I am just gathering up the most notable thoughts and experiences I have each day and week. So once you have a rough manuscript in your hands, it is already of great value because it is part of you and will remain as a record or legacy for you and others. And it has already paid off because it made you feel good.

Bringing a book all the way to ready-to-read form will probably cost you $15,000–$20,000 if you self-publish: $5,000 for art or illustration, $5,000 for printing, $5,000 for editing, research, and other expenses. Is this something to lose sleep over? I don't think so. Because this is a one-time expense, and now you have (if you printed five thousand or so books) $50,000–$70,000 worth of inventory. This is money that you'll earn back when you sell those books, especially if you sell them yourself (at lectures, seminars, or by direct mail). You *will* eventually sell them if you've picked a good subject, and that initial investment of $15,000–$20,000 has made you an authority—an author—which is more impressive to many than the $120,000 or more you may have spent on a college degree. And you have no overhead to eat you alive, just a little storage expense maybe. (If all else fails, you can borrow a basement somewhere.)

It's also just plain exciting to get something as awesome as your own book for only a one-time expense. Houses and cars drain you forever of time and cash you'll never get back.

A book is a real sword to cut a swath through life. It puts you in demand for speaking (and it will sell itself when you do). Books make people treat you well and trust you, too—people treat you better for being an author than they will for flexing any number of muscles from the gym, or winning the Grand Prix.

All these benefits explain why I now roll out three or four a year. Some sell a lot, and some only a little, but they all bring me wealth in some form or another. Which makes them a good investment!

Tools and equipment needed

Equipment is no excuse for not being able to do a book. You can take a book from zero to first draft without spending $50 on equipment and supplies (ink, paper, and scissors included).

I wrote this entire book on three legal pads with a Holiday Inn pen, by hand. I was in my jungle home in Hawaii (my typewriter there rusted out in one year). You could write yours on a 99 cent tablet with a #2 pencil.

Too many people get carried away with equipment waiting for the ultimate computer or software. "Boy, when I get a new typewriter, computer, recorder, Dictaphone, or software program, I'm finally going to write my life story or that great book."

That's like getting so engrossed in buying the ticket that you miss the plane. The abilities of computers and processors and copiers and other gadgets to produce print indeed incredible. You have options galore, but don't get bogged down in the mechanical aspects of it all. Remember, we are after the same end product that people were putting out in pre-Biblical times, or during the Lincoln/Douglas debates. It is the copy, the **content** that we need to stay focused on—technology is just a means to get us there.

(Do you get the point? Equipment doesn't write the book, **you** do.)

Good equipment, if you can afford it, can and will benefit you, especially when it comes to speed of corrections and redos. About a third of each of my books is usually written by hand—in motels, on airplanes, in cars, in church, at camp, during TV commercials, and in dull meetings. All of my box to rough manuscripts (see chapter seven) are done on a 1969 Olympic manual typewriter. From there they go on to computers for editing, copy reorganizing, spellchecking, typesetting, layout, and printing.

The bottom line here is, when it comes time to put your book into final form, if you haven't got a computer, there are thousands of used machines out there (fine for doing plain old word processing) that you can buy for a couple of hundred dollars. And there are many homebound computer trained people you could hire inexpensively who would weep for the chance to do a book!

The #1 secret of a successful book: YOU

Have you ever silently thanked the Lord that other people can't tell what you're thinking? Would most of us be in trouble or what? Our minds are magic, and our dreams are wild. Our minds just don't have the boundaries our more carefully considered and conventionally dictated actions do, and here is fodder for the finest book. You have the only earthly access to your mind, so its output is new, fresh, and, if presented right, fascinating.

The trouble is too many writers learned to write by doing research papers. That isn't writing. That is gathering, assembling, and organizing information (and often results in a mediocre message). "My paper," as the MBAs and PhDs call it, is often not their paper at all. It's homogenized parts of everyone—scholars who rounded up and quoted other scholars. Most such intellectual papers, truthfully appraised, are chloroform in print. The trouble with formal research like this is that it steers you away from **you**, and you is what usually makes a book good.

Sometimes, or most of the time, in my opinion, you should just write down what you have to say first, and shape, strengthen, reinforce, and decorate it later. Cutting down from the right raw materials will mean a tastier result than building up on hash and rehash.

I'm a real believer in drawing from oneself. This is new and fresh material that is much needed now. Why have more faith in others than you do in yourself?

> *Don't we always overestimate the abilities of others,*
> *and underestimate our own? Don't do it!*

The motto I live by here is "Go to yourself before the shelf." Dig the message out of you before you go out and try to dig it up somewhere else. Outside resources are great, but just make sure you use them as your secondary source.

CHAPTER 3

READY (Pick a Subject)
SET (Find the time)
GO! (Get Started!)

What should you write about?

When it comes to books, WHAT you write about is probably the most important question. I don't tell you this to scare you off, only to urge you to really consider and explore your "pick" before you buy a six-pack of notepads or a fresh disk for the computer. This is where most of your motivation will come from, your passion for what you will be writing about. It also has a big bearing on the ultimate profitability of the venture.

People will read almost anything if it's short (like a magazine article), has big headlines, lots of pictures, and happens to be lying around somewhere handy anyway. Asking them to read tens of thousands of words and pay five, ten, or twenty dollars to do it is a whole different story.

Think hard about what you intend to do with your book after it's finished. If you plan to sell it, why would anyone buy it?

In general, the more you can put in your book for the reader (as in "what's in it for me?"), the better. Everyone out there is looking for, and willing to pay for, a faster, better, cheaper way to do something, or to improve his or her present life situation.

Your book can be pretty personal or pointed—that will make it good. Just make sure you aren't the only person with that cause. If you pick the right cause or complaint (one that many people share) and let your book carry its banner, readers will rally to it because it's their cause, too! If you have the guts to get up and go with it, it's likely to make a strong book, and one that sells.

> *If you pick the right cause or complaint (one that many*
> *people share) and let your book carry its banner,*
> *readers will rally to it because it's their cause, too!*

Your cause can't be too narrow. Your fight to get a new streetlight out of the city council, even a victorious, funny, or sad three-year saga, isn't usually going to be a broad enough subject for a book. Your fight to get drunk drivers off the streets is a better contender because drunk driving tragedies have touched many lives.

One big question for a "cause" book is, do people want to be told what is good for them, or not? In general it is best to present the evidence and let them make the call. Overweight people aren't likely to buy a book telling them how dumb gluttony is, nor beer can flingers a book against littering.

A few more thoughts on the subject:

- When it comes to books, a good writer with a bad subject may go nowhere; a poor writer with a good topic has a much better chance. Readers will forgive a lot if the subject itself is compelling.

- It's usually best, and easier, to write about subjects you know well. As the Kingston Trio said way back in the 1960s, "It Takes a Worried Man to Sing a Worried Song." It's hard to write about things you haven't experienced, or things you've only casually observed, or a subject someone else has suggested.

- Do you have to be successful at something to write about it? Not necessarily—you might have learned just as much or more failing at it. Writing isn't an author's claim of personal perfection or of having all the right answers. Just some good ones that perhaps others have missed and that you would like to share.

- Does it matter if a subject's been done before, if there are other books on the subject? New books on cooking, fitness, sports, gardening, other popular hobbies, travel, and pets are done every year. And many of them sell and keep on selling. I've done fifteen books on cleaning, and others before me have done scores of others, but I'll never stop doing them.

Subjects can never be exhausted. What if no one wrote another book on politics, faith, sex, or cowboys after the first fifty were written? There are surely at least 5,000 new books on business every year, and 10,000 new books for children, and many more coming every year. If there are a thousand books out there on your subject, there is still only one **you** (and you will approach your subject all your own way). So you still have an advantage.

I had a friend who labored for years to get his little fast food business (a milkshake and hamburger stand) going. After years of fourteen-hour days that barely made him a living, he had almost reached the survival point. Then McDonald's moved in across the street. The fellow was ready to throw in the towel over it, but did his little stand do less business afterward? Nope, his business doubled. Then Wendy's moved in on the other corner, and both his and the Golden Arches' business improved. By the time Burger King appeared on the next corner, my friend's business had quadrupled. See the parallel?

- Not sure if you have enough to write about? Ridiculous! Every life is full of book ideas and possibilities. When people look at my many books and companies and projects and call me creative and brilliant, I have a good (and accurate) comeback: "I'm not really smart, just well exposed." And so are you!

- Don't be afraid to do something different. Don't be intimidated by all the experts (editors, publishers, advisers, etc.) out there who say "never" and "won't" and "can't" and "never has…" Your offbeat book idea might be just the thing to reverse all of those old book traditions out there. Until someone thought of it and tried it, no book ever came with a little bag of rice, modeling clay, or marbles to help children learn about grain, art, or how to play marbles, or included a CD or cassette or a fold-out map.

I've seen books with special ink on the cover that you touch to test your body temperature before you start reading and others with sound and participation features. New technology can complement a good imagination, so don't get hung on up just black ink on white paper, or paragraphs of plain type. When inspiration comes, be bold.

Too many "box" thinkers base their evaluations entirely on past history and their own experience. That is no guarantee and never any fun. To the risk takers go the biggest winnings, and the most experience for the next show!

> I'm constantly asked, "How can you write so much?" (five books now on clutter, and more than thirty books altogether so far).
>
> The easy answer: I clean up behind people and travel. That's all I need!

Fiction or nonfiction?

Don't get hung up on this—good books often conceive and deliver themselves. Concentrate on your message and your goal. Whichever (fiction or nonfiction) will accomplish or carry it the best, and you most enjoy working on, is the route to take. You might even switch in the middle of a book when you decide to add some fantasies to an otherwise dull story. That might make a better book than the nonfiction you started out with. You'll know!

If you have a wild and untamed imagination or are the world's first idealist and romantic, fiction will probably suit you. All of my books so far are factual nonfiction. However I have in mind a TV miniseries based on a fictional love story that I'm going to get to work on one of these days. It's based on a true story, but I need to embellish it some and change the names. I want to win a Pulitzer Prize with it. So watch the bookshelves!

If the book you have in mind is too racy for your real-life persona or profession, you might use a fake name, or pseudonym.

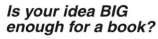

Is your idea BIG enough for a book?

There's nothing worse than trying to make a too-small subject into a book. You don't need to. If you can say everything you have to say in a pamphlet—your whole message—then keep it pamphlet-size, or make it a chapter. Most writers have tried this sometime—to expand a simple little idea or principle into a full-size volume, and it's just plain dumb. Good writing is uncluttered writing—adding decorations and extras to bulk something out that should stand alone on its own merits is not the way to get repeat readers. I've done books of all sizes, but I've also done a dozen or so little brochures and booklets, which I like and make good use of at seminars and speaking appearances.

If you have many individual essays or write newspaper columns, keep them all carefully filed and organized, and before you know it, you'll have enough for a book.

Too long... reader gone

On the other hand, people do pay attention to the thickness, or length, of a book. It started back in grade school and went on up through college, that first look at the size of a big, thick textbook. "Gads, do we have to get through all that?"

There is no set length for a book. This is entirely your call. But the size of the eventual book does have something to do with the scope of the idea you picked at the beginning.

How much do people really want to read about your topic? This is for you to decide. If you know your topic, then you know the interest in it, and the type of people buying and reading it. A busy businessperson wants to get to the point and get the message and get on with their day, while a relaxed novel reader only smiles at a three-inch-thick binding. You need to consider the audience and make your decision. Big books sell, but so do little ones. My first bestseller, *Is*

There Life After Housework?, was (in its later editions) over 200 pages and cost more than $10. One day we decided to do a condensed version of it with the key information in it boiled down to 80 pages. We called it *Clean in a Minute* and sold it for $5. It was a nice, light little book to carry along with me and sell at seminars, and its basicness was very appealing to many buyers. It's sold more than 130,000 copies now, a healthy figure for a self-published book.

Get what needs to be there in your book, but don't pad it to impress readers. I wouldn't, for example, put "How to Simplify Your Life," or "Easy Shortcuts for the Kitchen" into a 550-page volume. As you plan your book, keep asking and answering yourself, How and where is this book going to be used? adjust the length to that. People want to feel they are getting their money's worth, but they also don't want to dedicate their lives to finding out how to raise and train a guinea pig.

> "I, like all writers, have my file of brilliant ideas. After a while you see everything through the strange prism of "Is this a good book idea? Can this be made into a book, or not?"
>
> —*Nicholas Bakalar,*
> *book editor and author*

The key BOOK POWER ingredients

1. What you like

Whatever turns you on, turns your energy up and loose—your book needs this.

2. What you feel

Never assume people feel exactly like you. They might feel what you feel, but HOW you feel it is all you.

3. Your area of expertise

You don't have to be the best to have an opinion. What you know or do successfully validates you well.

4. What intrigues you

Yes, you might be ignorant or a novice in some area, but it stirs your very soul. This is an electric current that can weld you to a subject and lead to wisdom and expertise in it.

GETTING STARTED

You have your book idea picked out—all you need to do now is get started on it.

"I'm going to write a book," "I would have," "I should have," and "I could have" just don't cut it! "I'm doing" and "I did it" are more like it!! (And more fun!)

And don't say "you're saving it." Too many collections of "to write someday" are preserved… until it is too late. What a waste, and disappointment, to save and save and collect and collect, and then never use any of this.

Here's a little test to separate the wishers and wanters from the willers—the writers!

1. Do I really want to write a book?

2. Can I let other entertainments and trivial pastimes go for a while and do this?

3. Do I know what I want to write about?

4. If no one supports me, can I still do it?

5. Can I market it after it's written? This will take some energy— and moxie!

There are three ways of handling life: dream about it, talk about it, or WRITE ABOUT IT! You really start living when you start writing!

You have to start somewhere, sometime

Until you get across the wish or want line, you'll never be a writer. Writers do one thing, they write. The big secret is making something appear on that sheet of paper. What is not as important as **when**, because once you get to it, it gets to you, and if you keep writing, you'll keep getting better and better. I had a friend who was a real cowboy— he loved animals and worked with them daily, on roundup and in the corral. He always wanted to be an artist, dreamed about it, and did masterpieces in his mind. But he wasn't an artist until the day he sat down and drew his first horse. Sure, it looked more like a stick horse than the ones he saw galloping every day with their manes flying in the wind, but he drew a horse again the next day, and then the next. The horses gradually became more recognizable and realistic, and with these "lessons" he kept drawing what he saw and felt, and trained his hand and eyes. Today, twenty-five years later, his horse pictures bring him $30,000 each and are admired all over. His secret? He started, and kept at it.

FINDING THE TIME

So many of us want to write a book, but we have dozens, maybe hundreds of other plans and projects, things to fix, things to check out, things to take care of, books to read, things to invent, visits to make, trips to take, fun we'd like to have. Right now our brain is swimming with want-tos, need-tos, and should-dos.

I wake up in the morning amazed to find myself at "retirement age" with a much longer "to do" list than ever, and the knowledge that it's only going to get more exciting, there are more demands coming!

We may think we have "no time" to take on a single thing more in our loaded life. But we always can and do find time for the things we really want to do. If you want to write bad enough, you can and will make the time to do it.

What is the **main reason** we procrastinate writing? It isn't time, schedule, workload, health, or wealth (or lack of same). It's that

WE JUST DON'T WANT TO WRITE
BAD ENOUGH

Anything you really want you find a way to do or get, don't you?

If you are going to be a writer, having a story to tell isn't the problem. We all have plenty of stories, probably better than most of what's "out there," but we have got to want to tell them bad!!!

You will never just **find** the time to write, even if you are retired or unemployed for a while. You will only *make* time to write. Writing won't ever be #1 unless you make it #1.

Writing isn't a "stop life and do me" thing. Writing fits right in with regular life. It's a simple matter of capitalizing on what is going on already.

THERE IS ALWAYS TIME TO WRITE. You write **during** busy, not after or before it. You write during the battle, not after! You don't have to choose whether to write or fish—you can write while you fish!

Just for a challenge and a convincer, next time other pressures seem to be peaking, on your busiest day ever, write as much as you can. Surprise! Do it again! When is a better time? Your best stuff will come in the passion of doing, not "later" when you try to remember it all.

How I find writing time

People often ask me, "How do you write so much?" I write all of the time, everywhere—while traveling, speaking, eating, sitting in church, showering, even in bed. I don't like a rigidly scheduled writing life, and it doesn't fit the pattern of my other responsibilities. But I make the

most of every moment.

This morning, while working on this book, I got up at 4:30 AM in a Best Western motel in Fairfield, Iowa. It was raining, so filming was delayed on the TV segment I was scheduled to appear in. I propped up the three pillows on the bed and—with no food, no music, and no interruptions—wrote until noon—seven and a half hours of pure, free time and more than thirty pages "in the can." Yesterday, on the eight-hour flight here, I wrote not just on the planes (in between brief naps), but while waiting for luggage and rides, all by hand on a yellow pad.

A couple weeks ago I had an afternoon free and planned to pound out a few pages on the old manual when I got a call from the Forest Service. Range cattle had tromped down a section of fence on the creek bottom and were running wild on the upper part of our ranch. Writing over? Not on your life! I loaded a small pad and pen along with the wire, posts, and shovel. Then deep in the pines on a wonderful evening, viewing deer and moose, I pounded in posts and came up with and wrote down ideas—actually more writing than I'd have done at the desk back home. I mention these examples to alert you to the fact that you can get ready to write, and actually write at any and all times.

If you want to write, you don't have to wait until you're on vacation or unemployed. You can write in time fragments, "down time," waiting time, and bits and pieces. The way steady daily progress adds up is like the miracle of compound interest, or watching a tiny drip of water fill a barrel… overnight!

I owe much of my best writing to airline cancellations (adverse conditions of one kind or another). If I didn't write in cars, meetings, motels, and hotels, I'd only have three books out, not thirty.

On Sunday, when in church, I can plainly see all kinds of things to make business more profitable, so I write about them there. When in a meeting or other business situation, I can see all the ways moral principles can be applied to make life better, so this is when I write my best church talks and religious articles.

I travel with at least five book projects at all times, even on an overnight flight or a one-day jaunt. Sometimes I never touch the stuff, but if the mood or opportunity is there, I'll have the wherewithal to act on it. Often I can do in one hour, snowed in or stalled somewhere, what would take a day in an office setting.

Taking your book with you in your daily travels will help you keep going on it and take advantage of some of your best inspiration and energy. When something is left home on the shelf or shoved into a file, it is out of sight and mind, not really part of your life.

How to set up a portable office

Whether you are a frequent flyer, drive hundreds of miles a month, or travel by train or subway, you will find many hours to work if you have what you need at your fingertips. With (or for that matter, without) the aid of modern technology, you can ewrite most anywhere. We can do almost as much on the go with a handful of tools as we can at home with a roomful of equipment.

I always carry a complete kit of writing supplies and materials with me—even on vacation and to games and entertainments. Get a briefcase, box, or whatever that will hold what you—not someone else—need to process your daily installment of work on your book. A well-equipped case can contain, with a little condensing, everything you need. Choose your own container (just make sure it will fit under the seat in front of you, if you're flying), and fill it with writing supplies. You can buy kits that provide all the office essentials in a handy travel case. Or make up your own such kit.

Mine, for example, is a large Halliburton case filled with

1. Lots of yellow legal pads (my favorite for writing drafts).

2. Scotch tape (I like it better than paper clips for attaching papers together).

3. Many pens, a couple of pencils, and some markers.

4. A ruler.

5. Scissors.

6. Rubber bands (big ones!).

7. An electronic thesaurus (the size of a deck of cards).

8. Ear plugs (essential for concentration en route).

9. At least a half-dozen of my latest book projects. This gives me ample inventory to work on at all times.

Businesses can be run and bestsellers written with just those nine things.

A FEW MORE THOUGHTS ON THE PORTABLE OFFICE

• You can make a desk out of anything (we only use about one-eighth of our desktop at home anyway). A clipboard makes a nice sturdy surface to write on.

- A voice-activated tape recorder is the safest way to take notes *while* driving.
- PalmPilots, little hand-size computers/organizers, can also be used to take notes and records thoughts while traveling.
- Laptop computers, of course, are versatile and can help you produce a professional-looking product. (But a six-pack of writing pads and a few motel giveaway pens are even more dependable, and much less stealable.)

"My purse is my 'portable office': stocked with stapler, staple remover, pens, pencils, a glue stick, correction fluid, a small knife, and a small calculator."

—*Jenny Behmyer,*
freelance writer

When is the best time to write?

I can capture notes and ideas in the midst of noise, action, and hubbub, but when it comes time to put it all together masterfully, I need quiet, and I mean quiet.

Your book doesn't need competition or distractions. I find the morning, from 4 AM to noon, the prime time to write or study. It's quiet then, and unworn wits work better and faster.

Early is also a great interruption-stopper. Ninety percent of the people in the world don't get up and going until at least seven or eight in the morning. At three in the morning no one interrupts you, not even the birds. Three hours now of totally uninterrupted time is worth ten hours of trying to get "it" done on the battle lines. People are impressed that I do this until I tell them I go to bed at the decent hour of 9:00 PM, so that by three or four I've had plenty of sleep. They say wow, good idea! What productive thing do most of us do after 9 PM anyway—eat, watch or listen to the news, or argue. Turn in early and get up early, and you'll win.

> I never do serious writing during tired times. Creativity and energy are burned off by then. I do life's chores when I'm worn down. My prime morning times get my writing hand and mind, but I take notes twenty-four hours a day.

Darn the distractions, full speed ahead!

The top writer's interrupters (avoid 'em!):

> visitors during working time
> a clock (that we watch instead of watching our progress)
> food and drink and fiddling with same
> noise, from barking dogs to radio and TV
> phone addiction
> Internet and email addiction

Too many people are like a sounding board, a broadcasting bureau, a social confession booth, or a blanket-sized crying towel for the world and aimless friends. Tolerate this and your precious time will be stolen away by trivial matters, for the most part.

"Phone clutter," for example, often steals half our writing time from us. I do most of my writing away from a telephone, and that is one reason I sometimes get several books out a year.

Have someone else answer the phone. If you are alone, use the answering machine, and attach a notepad to the door. You could even resort to telling people you are going out of town so they don't call or visit.

I sometimes close the gate entrance to my ranch

even when I'm home and hide the car in the garage. Amazing how many "urgent" things take care of themselves and how efficient people can be about getting back with you some other time.

The secret of making sure you get your book done
(YES, THERE IS ONE—1!)

Like most of you reading this, my love for writing didn't start today or yesterday. It started way back in childhood or high school when a tiny thing or two, a single page or poem perhaps, pricked you, and gave you a sense of the power of words, of something that is written down. That single little seed never died. Maybe it waited until the kids were older or college over or whatever to sprout, but the want, the need, the destiny to write lives in you, and you know you'll never be satisfied until you write something, minor or major—you just have to do it.

Like you, I did plenty of school papers, letters, a poem or two, essays in college, and I waited for the recognition any of it would give. Finally I wrote and submitted a couple of articles to magazines on a subject I was really up on—efficient maintenance. I got a $25 check for one that appeared in *Telephony* (the magazine for telephone professionals). Gadfrey—I framed the letter that came with the check!

I was now a professional writer, hungry to learn more from the big boys (whomever they might be). Then a miracle—really just an ad on a bulletin board I walked by every day. A "writers workshop" was to be held that weekend at a nearby university, and there was a list of some of the things we would learn. I sent in the little card with my check, cleared my schedule, and by Friday was sitting in an auditorium with many other would-be writers, all trying to look intellectual.

We were a breed unto ourselves, every shape and size, all of us nervously sizing the others up to get some perspective on who was there—the competition. The host rose and welcomed us, and told us how lucky we were to have Tex Smith, a renowned writer, as our workshop leader. By the time she finished introducing him, we were all convinced this was almost the second coming. Then a casually dressed, rather ordinary-looking man in his forties got up and faced us. We were a little disappointed, but we held our breaths. He was one-half Cherokee Indian, wore his Levis like a cowboy, spoke with a drawl, and quickly got us involved by asking, "How many of you in here have ever had an article published?" There were three hundred of us "wanna bes" there, but only about twenty hands went up. We "pros" who'd raised our hands quickly gave arrogant glances at the lowly folks sitting around us who'd never had a byline. We were watching them squirm when Tex put all of our experience into perspective with the next question, "How many have had more than one article published?" That, in one fell swoop, eliminated all but two of us, who still sat there, beaming with triumph. "How many have done more than five?" he said next, and all hands were down. A murmur went through the audience—we were now all back in our place, a bunch of eager amateurs. It was then that I learned the one lesson, the single priceless principle of writing as a woman in a $100 hairdo and $600 dress asked, "How many articles have YOU had published, Mr. Smith?" Our leader was on the witness stand now, and he scratched his head and said, "Gosh, I guess about three or four hundred a year." A chorus of gasps followed, but the elegant woman didn't lose her composure. In her cultivated voice she now asked, "How do you account for such prolificacy, Mr. Smith?" Without hesitation he gave the answer—"A tired butt!"

I could have gone home after that three-word statement and had my money's worth. All of my publishing experience since that day has only confirmed the fact that talent, timing, contacts, media attention, editing, covers, marketing, and all of those other "musts" for a book count, but that "tired butt" rules. Persist, keep at it, and you'll get good at it. Trust Tex!

CHAPTER 4

Gathering the Material for Your Book (Collecting, Dissecting, and Selecting!)

The minute we decide to do a book, we start worrying about what's going to be in it and how it is going to get there. Both of these are actually rather simple. Collecting the ingredients is fun, and shaping and placing them is no big deal, either.

Before we start here, remember something I said earlier. One problem with school, especially at the university level, is that it encourages and even instructs us to assemble information and "research" from others and repeat it, instead of first finding what's in us. How often in reports, presentations, papers, speeches, and sermons, does the author start by quoting something from some learned person back in history or someone in the news today? This is okay, but way out of order.

Material from others—great intellects or the experts—should support your stand, not take it. Too many writers get so research happy they lose ownership of their work and it becomes an assembled summary of rehashed stuff.

Remember, I'm showing you how I do it, giving you principles you can adapt to your own situation, topic, and personality. This is "a way," not "the way."

Collecting

First, don't set up time lines or deadlines. They never work and end up getting you to work for them, not your book. When you start and finish is not all that controllable when it comes to books. Just go to work on it as fast, well, and smart as you can and let it come out when and how it may. Often something you thought would take weeks ends up taking only hours or even minutes once you get on a roll. Then some simple statistic or piece of art you were going to pick up, or page you were going to write in minutes, takes months. Deadlines are a false controller that divert you from writing to racing. Some books you can bring to a boil in a morning, and some books come slow. Letting them simmer as you gradually add ingredients will eventually make for superb reading.

I started a book called "How to Clean When You Can't Reach the Floor" (on cleaning with mild or major handicaps) more than a dozen years ago now, for instance. I've gradually made it broader, titled and retitled it, gathered information for it from experts of all kinds, and written on it every week for the past twelve years, and it isn't done yet. But it will be someday—and dynamite.

And those two books on outdoor recreation I mentioned earlier, "50 Games You Can Play Without Equipment" and "101 Scrumptious Skits for Groups," still aren't done, but every week or month, every camping trip, I find one more game or skit and chuck it into the "50" or "101" drawer. I just keep collecting and adding ingredients.

The roundup

A box or drawer is best for this. You can't see what's in files easily, and it's difficult to find and pull them. With a box or drawer, it just takes a second to toss something in. If you have great material that starts running over the box, what then? Start another box. Make sure every box or drawer is well labeled.

For filing raw materials for books, I often like to use metal cabinets with 4- to 6-inch deep metal drawers, one drawer per project. This way I can easily accommodate even bulky things like books and booklets in my "gatherings" on a subject.

What goes in the box or drawer? Everything related to your book:

1. Your notes

You have all kinds of thoughts about your book. Write them down (in a notebook or whatever you have handy at the time). Just be sure to capture and keep them, every one!

2. Clippings

Anything interesting you see in newspapers, magazines, newsletters, or programs. If it contains information on your subject or triggers an idea, rip it out and toss it in.

3. Comments

You'll hear comments that relate to your book from three-year-olds, doctors, lawyers, friends, winners and losers. Get them down, with the name and date. Outsiders' views of your subject can enrich your book and make it better.

4. Statistics relating to your idea

How many? How often? How big? How little? How bad? How good? Get it!

5. A page

You may write a full page or two, or just a paragraph on some part of your book, often brilliant. Toss a copy of this in there, handwritten or typed—keep it with the rest of your book fodder.

6. Ideas for illustrations—drawings or photos

If you see a photo, a sketch, a cartoon, an ad, or a layout—any illustration or graphic that might help get your message across—grab it and toss it in your box.

This rounding up or collection process can go on for as long as necessary to get a boxful of ingredients. Remember, most writers don't do it like they do in the movies, where a dashing young man or woman finds a remote beach or cabin and just sits down in a beautiful setting for six months or so and churns out a book. A novelist with a nonstop imagination might go about it this way. But the majority of us build our books out of parts, and we always collect more parts than we need. When you are looking, you will find!

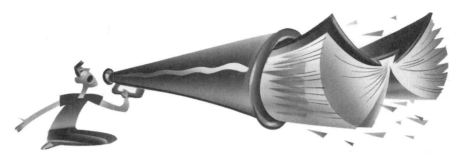

SHARE now... no secrets!

Some people get so paranoid about "their book" it's almost amusing. They slip around with that manuscript held tightly to their chest, afraid someone is going to steal their book or idea. This seldom—almost never—happens. I've found that one of the best ways to boost the collecting process is to make your path public. Let interested people know about your book, what you are doing, and why. Instantly you'll have scores of helpers and disciples with experiences, opinions, and comments, many of which are of great value.

Let me give an example from a book I'm working on right now.

One day I was at a gathering where several people were trying to give their teens away to any takers. Then someone said, "Don, you didn't have any trouble with your kids, did you?" I had good kids, from when they were little until now—they've brought much joy and satisfaction to my life. But there was one problem I did have with them. Like most people, I never felt very wise or smart about the way I gave my kids money. I always struggled with it—sure, they came out okay in the end, but there were some unnecessary pressures and stresses along the way.

So I swung the conversation into "giving kids money" and had an instant chorus of woes and groans and opinions about allowances and what unappreciative little buggers kids in general were these days. I jotted down a few notes and thought, "Hey, this would be rich material for an article or speech someday." Two weeks later I was in a meeting with my banker, and he told the group how poorly the average person handles money left for them by relatives. In other words, leaving kids money was one of the bigger problems in families, and ended up only a bigger hassle in estates. I took the brochure he offered on the subject, and my notes, and tossed them into the box I'd started on "How to Give Kids Money."

A month later I went to a business lunch with a CPA, and he mentioned some problems he'd encountered setting up trusts and inheritances—how and what to leave family was often the biggest problem people of substance faced. I brought up the fact that I was thinking about doing a book on this subject, and he offered to buy a dozen right then. This was a clear signal that there was a big need here. From the time kids are two until they are seventy, a parent has to provide them money in some way, and how this is done can help or hurt them for a lifetime. Obviously, you could write a whole book on how to give kids money.

So I continued the collecting process just as I've described it—no time limits, no pressure. I just began looking and listening for everything relating to kids and money. I remember a big dinner at a convention in Las Vegas—the table was loaded with famous people, business barons, movie stars, PhDs, and me the janitor, the keynote speaker for the convention, who remained silent as my tablemates talked over every social problem known to man. Finally one of the women there turned to me and said, "Oh, Mr. Aslett, I love your books. Are you doing any more?" "Yes, I am," I said, setting them up for the kill, "and the most interesting one is 'How to Give Kids Money.'" It was like tossing fresh meat to a pack of hungry dogs. Instantly we had a fired-up exchange. Everyone had the same problems and plenty of disaster stories. Writing under the table as fast as I could, I discovered that fistfights could easily break out over this subject, that no husband and wife agree on it. And the "multiple layer" families so common today (after each partner has more than one marriage, and then exes and stepchildren) only make things worse.

For years since then, I've been picking up sad stories, horror stories, even suicide stories, all from people who gave money unwisely. Do I have a firm cause and reason for a book! Everyone needs that book, and it can and will improve family harmony, save marriages, and help shape lives. I have hundreds of opinions now from all around the country on what we did and didn't do right with our kids, from plain ordinary people and filthy rich ones. The collecting has been fascinating, and all because I made my path public. Even if someone steals my idea, he cannot steal my personality and presentation of the material. And so my book, like your book, is safe.

> When you are working on a story, book, or presentation, don't be a silent collector. Be an open-mouthed one—tell everyone what you are doing and why and encourage them to contribute. Many will, and when they do, GET IT DOWN!

This box is pretty full now—I have articles, notes, letters, brochures, snippets of conversation, and bits and pieces of manuscript—nearly enough for a book. I haven't spent much money getting all this, and only a few hours. But it's super research, and all my own. I didn't have to go get it—it came to me, as I was going about my regular daily activities. I am lacking still some strong solutions—there are plenty of people with questions, but few with real answers for what to do in this area. Everyone has had the problems and agrees we need to correct them, but the HOW is seldom covered, and that is why this book is still in the works. Although there is plenty of material in that box, I'm looking for more realistic remedies. Once I have them, it will take me only a few days to organize the material and fit it into a nice and profitable book.

I have approached all the books I've ever done the same way. And I have material I'd never have if I just sat down at my typewriter and began to write. Every time I have an idea for an illustration, or someone tells me about a child who is begging them to cosign a loan, I jot it down and toss it in the file. Any thoughts I have on how I am going to sell this book and to whom go in there too.

Toss things in in rough draft form, if necessary, but clearly identified, so that you can activate or perfect them when you need them—maybe later that day, tomorrow, or a month or year from now.

When you feel inspired to write, you can dip into the box or drawer and pick out a piece of the subject and write on it. You can do a page, a chapter, or whatever, and toss it back in the box when you get bored or your favorite movie comes on TV.

The box is portable—you can take it with you. Many times when my mind is too tired to do anything astounding, I pull out all the little scraps and slivers of paper in there and type them up on a full-size page, leaving a three-inch space between them. That cleans up the drawer, condenses things, and jogs my memory of what is in there.

Then I copy the ten- or twelve-page transcript of my notes and stick a copy back in the box and carry a copy around with me, and add to or revise it as the spirit moves me.

That's really it. You have all the rest of what you need in your mind and your original impulse to do the book. All this has done is get you some additional angles, some ideas to flesh out, to enrich and broaden your subject.

If you are a good hunter and listener, and capture everything that stirs or amuses you on your subject, you'll have your book half done by the time you start to write it.

Can one pen do ten?

You can work on two books at once, or even three or four or ten. Oh yes you can!

Rarely does a true writer write just one book—most of us will end up writing several. Different things appear for different books on different days, and they can all be filed each evening in seconds.

At the moment I have eighty-seven separate boxes and drawers, each for a different book. Gathering for as many books as you want is simple, and you can do it without a glitch. You can work on two or twenty books at once this way, easily—just as you could remember the faces and names of twenty different students, twenty different ballplayers on different teams, twenty grandchildren, or twenty friends at a party. You just need to pick up the information, be it one page or one word, and at home, in the evening, toss it into the right box. And it will be there when you spread out that box some day.

Get it down!

The art of capturing good contents for a book is the most indispensable writing skill of all. You can't just sit down at a keyboard and bang out great material from even a good idea about a good subject. It has to have a spark of realism, and that doesn't come from just massaging the message, or brilliant word use. It comes from those short one- or two-sentence bits of real life you've captured in the thick of living. Those off-the-cuff appraisals, bits of criticism, humor, and philosophy you or others come up with that really hit the target.

The art of capturing good contents for a book is the most indispensable writing skill of all.

I hope I've made it clear by now that you should be writing all the time, not just at a set-aside time in your little writing space. Write ALL THE TIME, 24/7, as they say, every single place you go—while traveling, eating, working, dreaming, playing, in bed, and in the shower. You don't stop life and start to write, you write while you are in the midst of life.

The best quips come fresh from the lips, not while you are sitting on your hips at a computer trying to remember or think up something.

Every impression or interesting expression is gold to a writer, so capture, capture, capture. Capture everything. Don't let any thought, conversation, idea, clipping, or offer of help— anything concerning what you are writing about—escape. You'll have a hard time recalling later what you didn't record.

What you write on and with is your call. I'm never without the means to write—on the bulldozer, when out running, or going to church. What I cannot snatch up already typed or printed in its entirety, I write down. I use yellow pads, pieces of 2 x 4, the hood of the tractor, the palm of my hand, the backs of envelopes, and the margins of newspapers. I've even, in desperation (when a thought came to me while camping) written on a hard marshmallow.

Get it all

Get even the wildest ideas down on paper, any way you can, as long as it's readable. When someone hits you with five thoughts or concepts about something you are interested in, or you think of them or read them somewhere, don't stop and sort and measure and evaluate them now. Get them down, **all of them**, because

1. Some of what seem like the silliest ones may evolve into the strongest, freshest, or funniest parts of your book.

2. When you stop and start weighing or editing one, two, and three, you'll forget or lose four and five.

Do it NOW

"Now" has intensity that will show up in your writing. The reader can feel what really happened if you get it down *when* it happened. So I encourage you again: Write in the heat of battle (happiness, discouragement, or depression). Get it down while it's crisp and fresh, not from dreams, before it happens, or from half-healed wounds left afterward. Write during the pain or joy—if you wait, even hours or a day, you will lose the edge, so see it, taste it, feel it, and write it now. It's much easier and more efficient, and the results will be much better.

The same is true of material you gather from others. No point in saying, "Wow, was that good—I'm going to write it down" if you don't get around to it. So get it down now, in detail, at the very moment— exactly what was said and how it was said. We might remember the incident or information later to write about it, but we won't get the life or spontaneity it had when we heard it for the first time.

If you doubt this, the next time someone comes out with something with real impact, grab your pad (your pen should always be in your hand if you're serious about writing) and write it down, and then ask that person to repeat what they just said. Few can—they may give you the same information, but not in exactly the same form as the first time.

I can't emphasize enough the need to get those conversations, thoughts, or sudden glimpses down immediately. I don't care if you're running a jackhammer, and the notes you jot look like part of a Chinese menu. Get it down, don't worry about spelling or what you record on or where—in the tub, on the tour, or in a fit of passion, stop and get it!

Catching the snatches: "I always carry a little spiral-bound notebook in which I write snatches of things that I overhear and like. I travel by bus a lot, and you hear some great arguments, insults, and compliments, and jokes. I know what to do with humor, but rarely can think of any myself, so I find this very useful. I also collect 'looks' and mannerisms from people I see (and you need a lot of these for a novel)."

—*FRANCES SPATZ LEIGHTON,*
author of many bestselling
"as-told-tos"

"My mind is unbelievably prolific in generating ideas for stories and books; wherever I go I see possibilities for a dramatic development or a situation that could be explored…. Where do these ideas originate? From the workings of a fertile brain, from listening to the conversation of interesting human beings, and from speculating on the state of society. And some are of such force that they seem to insist on being put to use in the writer's work."

—*JAMES A. MICHENER,*
who needs no introduction!

If you want to be the best and cut the time it takes to do a book, read what it says in the section above again and DO IT.

Transfer it now!

Your notes and roughs, made on the run or anywhere, are the heart of your book. If you don't get them transferred as soon as possible into something more readable, you'll lose or forget them. This is especially true of abbreviated, hand-scribbled notes you captured quickly.

Losing anything (any of your precious ideas or sentences) is nothing less than life-threatening to a writer. It's a disaster, mentally and emotionally, as well as time-consuming. Losing some inspired bit of writing will turn you into a raving lunatic looking for it, and then ten days of depression after you admit that it's gone. Don't go through all that.

What's the worst thing that can happen to a writer?
Having a brilliant thought or inspiration and then:
"LOST IT!"
Write it down before you lose it! And then file it!

I transfer all my notes onto a sheet the minute I get to a desk. Type them up on typewriter or computer, or even write them out in long-hand, but get them out of rough scribbles and shorthand onto a clean sheet. If for some reason they must be left in the rough, check them over and make sure you will be able to read them a week or a month from now.

Once I have those cleaner copies, I usually put them in order, and then staple or tape them together (I don't like paper clips because they fall off and get hung up on files and other papers). Then I put a copy in at least two different places, in case of fire or flood, and the third copy I carry with me… everywhere! I put my "office" copies in the box for that book. But these "file" copies are just a safety net to prevent worry. The one I carry with me is the one I add to and keep refining and working on.

I hate having my material hidden in files or in computers. When I'm working on a book, I want everything printed out. To me a manuscript, when it is in the computer, still doesn't exist anywhere. I want it as hard copy, duplicated, within arm's reach so I can cut and paste and rob and alter. For this I use trays and boxes, and lots of Scotch tape, paper clips, and staples, plus large markers.

Make sure it's marked!

Be sure anything and everything you pick up is marked and identified so you'll remember what it's intended for and what it means. Too often we go back and find a note marked "wow" or "interesting," and it's so brief we can't remember where or why we picked it up, or what it actually is. Write a key word or sentence on it if necessary to make why you nabbed it unmistakable.

Remember, not only should the files themselves be identified and labeled, but everything you chuck in there should be, too. This gives you double protection against loss and confusion.

Be sure to IDENTIFY things (label them clearly)
and then put them where you won't
have to hunt for them.

Often on one page I'll have six paragraphs for six different books, randomly collected as I listen and travel. To save time I draw a little symbol by each paragraph to identify where it goes. This way I, or any of my assistants, can put things in the right place after a quick glance. For example:

My "kids and money" book: K$

My autobiography: Bio

My upcoming book on "How to
   Get the Goosebumps Back Again":

Writing or notes for my cleaning company, Varsity:

Notes for my editor, Carol Cartaino: CC

Sort NOW, not later

I don't mix things and sort them later—in writing there is no efficiency in "later" when you'll find yourself combing through things to try to separate them. Any hunting really hurts you worse than a physical wound, and unnecessary digging is dumb.

Ideas, notes, clippings, and photos, are never a mystery or a problem if you identify them and place them in the right spot when you first lay hands on them. If you toss them in a pile and wait until later to sort and separate, you'll compound the task about ten times, waste tons of good writing time, and probably end up with some of them in the wrong place.

- Manila file folders are godsends. I use them by the gross. Write the contents in large permanent marker letters on the outside so you can tell what's in there from across the room.
- In each book file, I have a sheet with the name, address, phone numbers, fax numbers, and so on of key contacts on that project so I can grab it and have all the information on a project, including the correct spelling of names, in a flash.
- If necessary, copy your files or drawers of info for someone, but never lend them out. You'll be sorry if you do!

On gathering from others

I've described the informal way of gathering information from others. If you are going to enlist the aid of others in a more direct way, bear in mind that casual mentions and soft solicitation rarely works well. Like, "Hi, Harry, I'm writing this new book on the history of musk ox hooves. Do you ever go to Alaska?"

Harry: "Yeah."

"Well, if you happen to see any musk oxen, could you take an impression of a hoofprint or two, or maybe a picture, for my book?"

Harry: "Yeah, sure."

Well, you won't get diddly squat from Harry in the next forty years, even if he marries a musk ox.

Or: "Would you look this over when you get a chance, and tell me what you think?" This will often get you nothing, either, except wasted photocopies and lost manuscripts (although you may stimulate the person in question to write a book and ask you to help them).

Here is the right way to get help. Write a letter or memo to people you know are intelligent and energetic. Make the letter short, lively, and not too blatantly flattering, and ask them very specifically for what you want. "I'm writing a book on working in a home office, and I'd like to know exactly what YOU do, how you cope, when your computer suddenly goes down in the middle of an important assignment."

The last time I did one of these, twenty-four of the people I gave them to responded with wonderful material. You won't always get a good return from things like this. But even when the percentage of yield is low (often only one in twenty), there are usually a few gems in it all that make it worth it.

You can't achieve perfection without a good selection

Starting a book without rounding up and writing down your ideas and a gathering a good supply of material will be discouraging. You will run out of material and it's a real kick in the butt once you start writing to have to stop the flow and go "research" for something. So overkill on ideas and resources. Having overkill, too much, is always great. You can edit down much easier than you can find and fill.

When classical research is needed

For technical, historical, academic, and other books where more formal research and documentation is required, just follow those research basics you learned back in high school or college. And remember that dates, amounts, and places have to be exact, not abstract! For an up-to-the-moment primer on researching in an efficient and orderly way in the computer age, see chapter seven of my book *Get Organized, Get Published!*

"Research material is used to keep my stories historically correct. When I worked on my historical novel *Sacajawea,* I believe I read everything ever written at that time about her, the members of the Lewis and Clark Expedition, and the territory along the Missouri and Columbia rivers. As a family we traveled over the Lewis and Clark Trail, going to historical societies, museums, and universities along the way to collect ideas and knowledge in notebooks and on notecards. In Montana I lived next to the Lewis and Clark Trail, so that portion of American history was familiar to me. Sacajawea was my heroine.

Doing the research for my novel *Prairie,* we went to Cheyenne and Laramie in order to make chronological sense of, or organize, an Irwin family scrapbook comprised of clippings (with no dates or names of newspapers), poems, valentines, ribbons, and locks of hair. We visited libraries and historical societies in Wyoming, Colorado, Utah, Southern California, and across the

Mexican border in Tijuana, and interviewed family members who were close to the protagonist C.B. Irwin and the family Y6 ranch.

My novel *Circle of Stones* took us to Wales to do research about the twelfth-century expedition of Madoc, son of Prince Owain, who came to this country in 1170 AD. We visited universities and historical societies and the famous Folk Museum. Most people there knew the history of Owain Gwynedd and his mistresses.

As I continue work on the sequels to *Circle of Stones,* I am using the local library, interlibrary loan, the North American Welsh Newspaper, the Internet, and the U.S. Hydrologic Centers Defense Mapping Agency for oceanographic charts on ocean currents, passages, and world climatic sheets. I have been to Mobile Bay, where Madoc may have landed, studied anthropologic material on the Florida Calusa Indians, the classical Mayans in Yucatan, the Mound Builders in Illinois, and the nineteenth-century Mandans along the Knife River. And I have written to dozens of writers asking permission to use a sentence or two they wrote that is pertinent to my work as epigraphs for my chapter headings."

> —*ANNA LEE WALDO,*
> *author of bestselling historical novels*

"Whenever I get an idea for a book, I immediately make a rough table of contents, then create a file folder for each chapter. That way when I get a brainstorm, read an appropriate article, or find a good quote, I can dump it in the right file folder without further thought. When it's time to actually write the chapter, a wealth of material awaits me."

> —*MARILYN ROSS,*
> *author and consultant on self-publishing*

CHAPTER 5

GIVING YOUR BOOK A NAME AND FACE: TITLES AND COVERS

I'm going to interrupt the "how to" sequence here a bit to inject a little more fun and excitement into the process. Some things on a book have to be done early, often even before the book is fully written, and among those are titles and covers.

Take some time now for the title

Most of us have some ideas for a title even before we start a book. I had pretty firm title ideas for all thirty of my books before I wrote them. Only two are still on the books they started with. There's nothing wrong with that. You need a "working title" to start a book, but a "selling title" to sell it to readers or the bookstore, and publishers or others can help you find that.

I've been praised for my titles. Some I thought up, some friends, editors, or other publishing pros suggested, and some just popped out of a list of fifty brainstormed possibilities. But almost every title I have now wasn't a pretty process—it was a sometimes agonizing matter of shifting, experimenting, reasoning, choosing, compromising, rethinking, going back to the drawing board, and when you get to the bottom line—guessing and hoping. Generally you have to work at a title, because even those you think are great at first often don't match the full content or message of the book by the time you are finished, or have some drawback it takes an outsider to see.

So don't get hung up on your original idea or ideas. Start collecting a list of possible titles. This is valuable because some of these you'll end up using as chapter titles or headings within chapters. I have never, nor do I expect to ever, run into any title experts, and I've worked around and with the biggest and the best in book publishing. You are as clever as anyone else.

This titling business boils down to five major guidelines:

1. Tell what the book is about.
People get annoyed when a title doesn't fit or immediately tell them what a book is about.

2. Make the title catchy or attention-grabbing if you can.

3. The shorter the better.
If a title isn't easy to pronounce or slip into a conversation, people won't do it, and your book will be at a disadvantage.

4. Make some kind of promise, or suggest a solution.

5. Make the title easy to say.

So work at that title. No matter how long it takes, don't give up and accept anything mediocre just because you're tired of thinking about it or are desperate. Why should you work hard to come up with a title that is nothing less than the best?

Would the famous bestseller *Dress for Success* have sold millions if it had been called Proper Attire for Working? That first impression of your book is critical to its sale, can make or break it. If the title misses the mark, there goes all that work and money.

If, on the other hand, your title piques people's interest, they will pick it up to investigate or check it out further, and you have a much better chance of their buying it.

The bottom line: Good titles mean better sales!

The title of my first book really worked and had a big part in its million-seller success. *Is There Life After Housework?* was funny, touched on a problem (homemakers were really able to relate to it), and hinted at a solution.

The title of my second book, also very successful, used a common but slightly funny question to lead off a collection of cleaning questions and answers: *Do I Dust or Vacuum First?*

My third (and best ever) book was called *Clutter's Last Stand*. This said it all. It was funny, related to another famous demise (Custer's Last Stand), and again, promised a solution.

My fourth book came out while I was on the top of the heap—on two bestseller lists. This was a book to get men to clean—the topic and timing was perfect, and here was a real need. The text and artwork were brilliant, and all of us experts (me and the editors and marketing wizards at Writer's Digest) bought the title: *Who Says It's a Woman's Job to Clean?*

The book presold a record 70,000 copies (three times more than Mickey Mantle's book that year), and it received more interest from the media than any book I'd ever done… and yet the book was only "successful" rather than a full-scale bestseller. Why? The title was wrong. The audience was supposed to be men, yet that title was a little antagonistic toward them. And highly traditional women were put off by its boldness.

For my next several cleaning books, I strained and searched for a good title, but I couldn't come up with any. And then Jeff Campbell, a

Here is a spread of quick "title and cover tryouts" I did for a book on modern-day bad manners.

fellow professional housecleaner, did a little book much like my own first one and put a brilliant title on it—*Speed Cleaning*. There it was, in two words—a clear, clever, and compelling promise about a dreaded task.

Now, while you are still collecting the ingredients for your book, is the time to put a label on it—title it. The longer the list of ideas you come up with, the more you'll have to choose from and the better you'll do in the end. One will "click" and stand out from the others. So don't get stuck on your first swing—get all the suggestions you can. Often you are too close to the topic to call it right. It will be fun to work on titles. Write them down, share them with people, and watch their responses. Or get a group going on the problem.

Good titles are out there somewhere, and finding one is important.

Something I love to do that can help here is to put together a whole page of different titles (complete with rough cover designs for each). This gives me a quick overview of how my different title ideas might actually look on a book and helps me see which have more clout and presence.

The cover

Now is also a good time to come up with some cover ideas. The old adage "you can't tell a book by its cover" is simply not true. The cover projects your book's character, personality, and identity. It helps readers recognize your book and is often the key to getting them to pick it up and open it up. But often, here, too, it takes a lot of trial and error to come up with a good one. When I've put out feelers or requests for cover experts, I find no one coming forth willing to stake their lives or reputations that "this will work." So here again, it's an open field, and you are as good a player as the next guy.

Here are a few of the covers proposed for my first big seller, *Is There Life After Housework?* We went through more than three dozen ideas over the years and the different editions of this book, and few of them were ever used or even liked by most of us.

Below right is one of the rough covers chosen and submitted by the "experts." We thought it was a joke, but they were serious.

For the "Tenth Anniversary Edition" we used the cover at right. The background was a nice bright yellow, like the original edition.

Just when you think you're getting good at covers, you discover there is something else to learn. The cover of our twentieth book had a handsome, shiny purple background. It looked great, but showed and magnified every fingerprint.

The "Big Three" of covers

What are the BIG THREE when it comes to covers? A cover needs to be:

1. *As simple as possible.*

2. *Colorful/attractive.*

3. *Distinctive—easy to identify. A rule of thumb in the book business says you should be able to read, and recognize, a book cover from across the room.*

If you are published by a publisher, it will have control of the cover and very strong opinions about it. But you can and should have your own ideas and not hesitate to advance them and argue for them.

If you are self-publishing, you can put any cover on your book you want. Don't wait until two days before the presses are due to roll to come up with it. Start right at the first, or in the middle of your book.

Start thinking early about the cover, including that key selling copy that will appear on the back cover of your book if it is a paperback or the flap of the jacket if it is a hardcover.

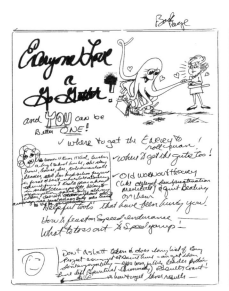

*From my handwritten rough above
left to the typed rough beside it, to
the later versions below, the back of
a book can have many evolutions.*

Here are back covers from some of my books.

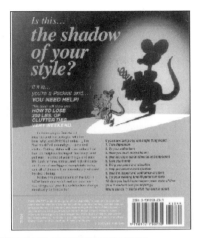

The back cover of a book (especially today, when so many books are paperbacks) is one of your most important selling tools. Start early to think of copy and visuals for your back cover that will turn browsers into buyers.

I often do my own "stick people" roughs of some cover ideas, and then have an artist do some better roughs of these, plus his or her own ideas for a cover. Then I have the artist do a more finished rough, in color, of the one or two I like best. All of these cost something, but I believe it is money well spent. See chapter ten for more on covers.

What I gave the artist:

Artist's pencil rough:

Artist's color rough:

Artist's cover idea:

Final cover:

Some of the many title and cover attempts for my "new century cleaning book," No Time to Clean*!*

The title and cover we finally chose.

CHAPTER 6

WRITING IT!

After writing three bestsellers followed by three intense media tours and reading all of the press releases, reviews, and articles on me and my book that resulted, it became clear to me that many of those other writers (newspaper, magazine, and advertising copywriters) were much better writers than I was. Especially the newspeople—they could cleverly and accurately summarize my whole book's message in a single column of type. I'm always amazed at how good the newswriters are, in even the smallest town. I ask them why they don't write books, because they surely could outdo most of us "authors." "Can't do it," they say. This intrigues me, as I receive many comments like this from other good professional writers as well. And it got me to thinking about the difference between book writing and other writing.

A book is a long-range undertaking in every way. You don't write a book overnight, and you wait longer for results after you do get it written. Books take more space in your mind and shelves than shorter forms of writing and probably ten times the organization. The pressure of outcome on a book is greater, too. An article is generally a part of something larger, such as a magazine, while a book has to stand alone, on its own. Books are more entrepreneurial, while some other kinds of writing are more "team" or social.

While books don't take any more, or even as much skill to actually write, they do take more planning and processing. Books are also a much greater investment of time, and thus much more of a gamble.

So if you write well and want to write a book, it's fun and just requires a little more long-range perspective and planning, and don't forget patience. Books take longer, but they last longer and bless you and your wallet longer, too. (And those article writers and columnists could just keep their fifty-two essays a year and after a few years sort and arrange them and bind them together into a book!)

Working from the vision back

I start from a totally different end of writing than most people. Before I write much, or even a word, I visualize the work completely finished, the pages laid out and printed up, the book complete with artwork and covers, everything. And I see myself publicizing it all over.

Likewise, when I look at the forty acres of forest, brush, and creek on which my partners and I intend to build a nice girls camp, and before a single bush is cut, I see the entire park finished

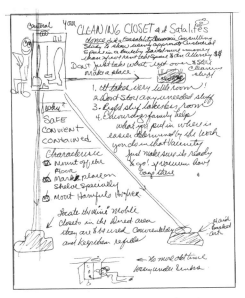

I design and illustrate my books from the beginning, from the very first rough draft.

and being used. I see girls jumping and running and playing volleyball on the court we will build. I see the picnic grounds and the playground and see those girls bringing their own daughters there to play someday.

So when I do a book, I don't just write it, I do a cover for it, illustrate it, and lay it out as I go along, right in the first draft. I hate plain pages of double-spaced manuscript. They just aren't alive for me. Book editors and English teachers love a manuscript done the traditional way, but I think it dulls the senses. When I do my rough (which is far, far from a finished book), I want it to look almost like a finished book. I have to write from the vision back, not from the inspiration up. Seeing see my dream clearly, in Technicolor, helps make it come true.

How to write compellingly

Ever notice the difference in people who are reading books? Some carry a book around forever, dipping into it a little at a time here and there. Others labor to "get through" a book they paid good money for. Others abandon books half-finished, promising to get back to them later (a later that never comes). Then there are the books people don't just read but devour—they can't put them down, forget dinner or read right through it, don't even feel the sleeping baby on their lap wetting through his diaper.

There are dozens of books out there on how to write compellingly. My boiled-down advice on this again is as follows: Pick a subject that you know and like, or better yet, have a do-or-die passion for. If you really feel your subject or message, even if you aren't a gifted writer, you'll do okay. Your passion will give a bold edge or angle to the information that even the best grammar or style will never give it.

Know and love your subject and people will want to read about it, even if it happens to be "watching paint dry."

Some other things that help:

• Illustrations that liven up the pages.

• Including good stories and anecdotes in your book—people like stories much better than sheer logic, and they hold attention and bring points home better. Remember here: Draw on yourself before the shelf—your stories before Paul Harvey's—and your book will come alive.

• Lists and charts and the like are easier than page after page of straight text for today's readers to assimilate. There's a reason "tips" are so popular.

Being clever, including alliteration and figures of speech in writing is great, but this is like salt in a good soup. Enough is enough—you can metaphor a manuscript right out of meaning!

Let the reader take part in your book

The most important advice I ever received about books was from Carol Cartaino, then the editor-in-chief of Writer's Digest Books, the company that does more books on writing than any other. In my opinion Carol is one of the best in the business and this bit of advice shows it.

"Don, notice that when people have a conversation, they learn from about the age of four on up that if they don't let others in on the conversation, let them have their say, they will lose interest in the conversation (and you, too).

Surely we all like to tell our story, our experiences, our opinions. 'Ours' is our favorite subject. This is only human. But if the other guy can't get some of his own experiences, opinion, and stories into the exchange, he'll lose interest. We all learn this in life (or should have) and practice it for a successful interaction with friends and associates.

But deep in our hearts still lurks that desire to tell and show our own stuff—we are all this way, even though we may be disciplined on the surface to control ourselves and share the stage. Many people, when they go to write their book, think, 'Aha, now at last it's all me!' And yes, you can write your story, your experience, and your opinions and lay all this on those readers out there. But writing for someone is not all that different from talking to them. If there is nothing in it for the reader, if he cannot take part in what you write, as he does in conversation, he will withdraw and lay down the book. You have to write like you converse and let the reader have his turn. Don't just tell him, include him."

SIX SIMPLE WAYS TO INCLUDE THE READER

1. Use the words "you" and "your" and "we" and "our," rather than "I" and "my," whenever possible. ("Now we are going to put our book together…")

2. Ask readers questions from time to time, or to summon up some aspect of their own experience with the subject you are writing about: "How many times have you found yourself without some key thing you need to do a job, and then wasted half a day trying to locate it?"

3. Make the reader aware, from time to time, that you know she has something to say about the subject, too: "As anyone who has children knows…" or "You've probably had equally dramatic experiences with your own escaped pets."

4. Include exercises self-rating quizzes or for the reader.

5. Localize examples and references whenever you can. We have a tendency to use media overworked famous places and faces for reference. Whenever possible (depending on the scope and focus of your book, of course) use local examples, or ones that are more directly connected to your readers in some way. Pick out a person, place, company, or event your readers can relate to more personally and intimately.

Always keep your audience in mind. If you're doing a book for people in the military, it's only logical to use military examples and anecdotes rather than farm or sports ones.

6. Use humor—laughing is a great way to participate!

Present, don't preach!

It's fine to present your position in your book and make the case for your point of view, but don't make the jury's decision. Pull any strings you can in your presentation—use logic and humor, appeal to good sense, compassion, or even greed—but let them tie the knots. It's okay to provoke, but not to preach ("you should, you ought, you better," etc.). Don't tell readers how to feel or what they ought to do. Present the information and let them draw their own conclusions. Being opinionated is fine, but getting judgmental will turn people off.

If you're writing on something technical

"If your writing involves explaining something technical to laypeople (as a plastic surgeon I must do this daily), it is incredibly helpful to try your explanations out on people orally, to see if they have any trouble understanding them. If your vocation and the subject of your book are the same, this is easy to do. Otherwise, you can utilize someone from your circle of friends and acquaintances who doesn't know much about the topic.

I've learned a lot from my patients this way about how to explain things."

—Dr. Jean Loftus,
plastic surgeon and author

Years of experience have taught me that when you need technical information or documentation, searching out an individual (the best in that particular field or specialty if possible) sure beats hunting through libraries and on the Internet. Sure the "paper chase" or "screen search" is fine for all kinds of general, background information, but when you find a person who knows and loves her profession, she will be the frosting on the cake. She will give you not just information, but the very latest and best with an opinionated slant, which can open up the human side, the moral side, the environmental side, or the humorous side. Most self-made experts are nice people who are eager to share their knowledge.

What order should you write your book in?

Many of us would be surprised if we were to watch a movie being made. When you watch the average movie, as when you read a finished book, it usually goes in 1-2-3 or A-B-C order. But putting a movie together that way would triple the cost. Often the end of the movie is filmed first and the beginning last. Moviemakers film where and when the cast members are available, and they shoot all the scenes at once for the locations that happen to be on set now. They have a script and know all the elements they need, but they do them when they are the easiest to do—which does not necessarily mean in order. Then, when all of the material is "in the can," they splice and edit and organize it, cutting some of the scenes in half but making them fit the whole. It's inspiring to watch these masters of organization work!

Likewise, you don't have to mentally lock into the idea of a book that starts, "When I was born…" or "In the beginning…" and goes straight through to today. You can write it in sections. I often don't start at the beginning and then do chapters one, two, and three. I do chapters and sections almost at random and way out of sequence when I am just in the mood to write certain parts.

The key here is to have an outline or clear idea of the whole structure and then use your own version of that little scissorslike clapboard moviemakers have labeled with the act, scene, or take. If you put something like this on all the material you write, even in wildly scattered bunches, you don't have to worry about figuring out where it goes later because big, plain labels will organize the material by itself. And if something doesn't fit, you can use the footage in another "film" or project. After all, it's your movie (you are the producer and the director, too!).

> *I don't start at the beginning and then do chapters one, two, and three. I write a book like the Hollywood people shoot movies, almost at random and way out of sequence. To the people around me it is murder, but I get the best manuscript this way.*

The button, or the old book? (two silent partners)

There's a lot to be said for the new automated versions of everything, especially when they help you get fresh ideas into motion instantly—no waiting often means good writing. I received one of those little handheld, calculator-size electronic thesauruses as a gift, for example. A compact tool like this is very convenient for carrying along with you. I use it often, especially when writing poetry or short pieces, to instantly get a supply of synonyms for the rewrite I usually do before I do my final copy. That little machine spoiled me, however—the ease of button-pushing got me out of the habit of pursuing **all** of the possibilities of spinoffs of words and ideas. Once when I was exploring a word and got maybe five or six corresponding meanings from my little electronic helper, the batteries went dead. So I reached up on the shelf and picked off my old faithful *Roget's Thesaurus,* and bonanza! I found more than fifty great related words. I'd forgotten how much was in there and how easy it was to use. The book might be a little bulky to take traveling with me, but when I'm doing serious writing in my home or office, it beats the 144,000-word electronic thesaurus four ways to Sunday. I always like to have ALL the possibilities before I sort them down to the practicalities. I use both types, but after I get my electronic list, I comb the pages of the thesaurus and always find more and better material.

Should you work on one book at a time, or more than one?

If you're working on one book and new ideas crop up, and they will (what a thrill!), what should you do?

Don't let any good stuff slip away. You don't have to stop one book to start another (or two or three or four more). Afraid you'll lose focus? I doubt it—as long as you have the passion for the big one or the initial one, you'll give it the most effort. If you don't, there may be a message here for you: Maybe you should drop the first big one and whip on the new one.

As I mentioned earlier, I'm working actively on ten books this year alone, twenty more that I will produce over the next couple years, and maybe sixty more book ideas for the next ten years. And I bet I'll get double that number of new ideas while doing it.

You could compare this to the different ways to water fertile ground. You can flood or sprinkle it. If you work on one book alone with all of your time and effort, that is a flood-time book, and great. However, to work on a number at once, to nurture them all with perhaps less intensity, we go to the sprinkler system. It sends out many tiny drops, continuously, hour after hour, which in the end penetrate the soil better and do the whole job of watering more gently, just as a soft, misty rain for three days straight will saturate the earth better than a big flood of water on a single day.

Sprinkling your ideas and efforts over ten different books will make them take longer, of course, but it is fun and you are less likely to lose enthusiasm for them. I get bored working on one book only. I get better results when I spread out my efforts over many projects. So don't worry when new ideas "distract" you—that's good. More options and choices just make things better.

Most good new book ideas come from working on another book.

Beware of "writer's block"?

I don't really believe in "blocks" of anything that is worthwhile and productive and that you really want to do. But there do come times in writing for all of us—new or experienced—when we wake up to the fact that although we are immersed in writing something and it is spread all over the place, we talk about it daily and worry about it hourly, yet it seems to be "on hold," to be going nowhere. Things seem to be backing up and slipping backward at the same time.

This is a critical time in writing a book, the time when most people put it away until "later" (until things get better, after the class, the

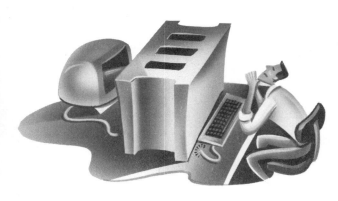

wedding, the trip, the funeral, the surgery, the job change, while they're in love, until retirement). Or they find some reason to back off for a while and "regroup." This is never thought of as an actual decision to abandon—just a delay to refresh yourself before diving back in.

This is death to a writer and where many books (with months and even years of work done on them) die on the vine. Their authors lose confidence and momentum, or get tired of explaining to all of the critics, and their family, why there is "no book yet."

In good book writing there is no later, it is now, now, now, no matter what. Writers don't wince at the weather or whine about a busy clock or calendar. That is all irrelevant to your book. In fact pressure, setbacks, criticisms, illnesses, or other adverse conditions should only enhance your writing. It's the old "when life hands you a lemon, make lemonade" approach.

I am a successful writer not because of grammatical skill or spelling, for sure. What's my secret? Keeping intensely involved in living, taking on more than I can handle, and persevering harder when times get harder.

You won't have any blocks in writing, you'll have all kinds of breaks, good and bad, and how you handle them—wasting them, waiting around, or moving onward—is what makes or doesn't make books. The Boy Scout program has taught me some great principles. The scout slogan, for example, is "Do a good turn daily." It doesn't mean if you feel like it, if it's convenient, if there is a need, or because you know you're going to be rewarded for it. It says do a good turn daily, period. There is no allowance for "good turn block." In scouting, likewise, the goal is to be an Eagle Scout, and like finishing your book, it is easy and entirely attainable if you just stick with the program. Yet only about four percent of the boys who join scouting ever get their Eagle. Should we blame this on "Eagle block"?

So don't let the down times become set-aside times in your writing—they don't need to be. You can write all the time, no matter what, do your best stuff during the worst of times.

Don't even slow to a walk when the writing seems to reach a "drag," "going nowhere," or "confusion" point. It's time to quicken the pace, and "Write a good page daily!"

The value of a rough... more than one rough

There are two things in writing I've never liked:

1. Straining for perfection

2. Erasers

Plodding, pondering, and pounding away to try to get a perfect draft of something when things just aren't flowing is worse than beating your head against the wall. "Grinding out" anything in writing may be necessary at times, but when you have to fill space without feeling, the end result—your book—suffers. Often you can write two or three quick, flowing versions of something in the same time a long, laboring one takes. And one of the three will often be outstanding. Going through the draft of my autobiography recently, I found three separate one-page versions of the same subject done years apart. One was super, and the other two, which contained the same information on the exact same subject, were no good at all.

There is value in doing two or three different drafts when something doesn't feel right or "zing." This is a principle that ultimately saves time and improves quality in anything. Building a good book is like building a good house. Doing models or mock-ups really paid off when I was finishing my low-maintenance home in Hawaii. When I wasn't sure which style of border to put on the ceilings, for example, I made up samples of four different styles of borders and held them up on the ceiling. The perfect one was easy to pick out then. Likewise, when trying to pick out the best color of floor tile and grout, I had little samples made up of nine different colors of tile and grout and then picked the best.

It's not a waste of time or money to overkill a bit if you are in doubt—having options, a selection, gives you freedom in writing and better quality. I don't like rewrites and erasing, but I do like overwrites—doing the whole thing over again and then having two to four options to choose from instead of one beat-up, overedited version. Doing an entirely new version is usually quicker than a labor-intensive rewrite. Time or mood can give you several different takes on the same subject, and one will always be better. I guess I'm an old farmer who's learned that every "litter" has it runts and its #1's.

The glory of writing… has some gory, too!

A few negatives do pop up (especially from the onlookers) when you bury yourself in "your book." The following tongue-in-cheek look

at the process from a less idealistic angle may prepare you for some inevitables and enable you to laugh a little as you surge on, undaunted still!

1. *No one, at work or home, will expect his schedule (your slave services!) to be altered because you are writing a book.*

2. *Your family will get tired of the mess, and of you hogging the mail, phone, Internet, and table space.*

3. *When you arrive somewhere, people will glance at your hands before your face, checking to see if you are still carrying that manuscript around.*

4. *You'll get sick of answering, "Isn't that book done yet?"*

5. *Your family and friends will begin to doubt your sanity.*

6. *Some will suspect that you have a secret life going on somewhere and are writing about it.*

7. *People will begin to counsel you about not losing your perspective on life.*

8. *You'll find that people have plenty of time to criticize but little time to help.*

9. *You'll begin to doubt your own memory as you try to recall whether you've already used a particular story or brilliant passage somewhere in the book.*

10. *You'll keep looking for, but rarely find, the glamor that is supposed to go along with writing a book. There is no slack and no pat on the back.*

11. *You'll make some people uncomfortable, some paranoid ("Where did you get that idea, anyway?"), and many envious.*

12. *You'll cause people to lie when you ask them how they liked your book (or if they read it).*

13. *A jealous streak you didn't know you had will bloom when other books sell and yours doesn't.*

14. *No matter what the cost or consequences of writing this one, you are already thinking of at least two others!*

My most important advice here is: Don't let others take over your book. Once you start writing, you'll hear every "you should," "you ought…", and "if I were you…" imaginable. And some of these may get you far afield from your original idea. Outside feedback is good, but don't let it become the core. Keep it strictly a contribution.

And last, when you get bogged down sometime, and maybe to doubting yourself and your whole book venture (the old batting slump effect), remember that this is the same as getting drowsy in the middle of an otherwise-exciting day. We all go through it, and we snap out of it. In the end, you will be glad, you will rejoice that you wrote YOUR BOOK!

HELP HELP Help! (The alone attack)

Several times during the siege of serious writing, you will be aware of being all alone in a big project. In most things these days, we have help deciding and doing. Assistance is all over the place, and we get used to logging on, yelling for help, getting aid from scholarships, grants, loans, rooters, coaches, spouses, and sponsors. There is help from all kinds of sources, even when we don't need it.

Writing, however, is pretty much a one-man show. They may get some outside help in things like research, but most writers are loners, as far as the actual authorship is concerned. The outcome of the project is in your heart and head, and it's usually hard to get a helper. In fact try for a little sympathy and you won't get much of that, either. There are times when your project or subject matter gangs up on you, usually when you are feeling less than confident, and you'll get a sudden, intense desire for help. Relax. Expect this, sleep on it, and generally it will go away. A little insecurity about your writing is a good thing, and isn't nearly as bad as it seems.

Actually getting some serious help—cowriting a book, or collaborating with a colleague to do it—can be good if you are selective. Four of my books so far have been coauthored, and luckily all three of the partners involved were the type who did more work than me. Generally the opposite is true. In several book ideas and starts I had with others, I found that enthusiasm declines fast from that first conversation. Weight pulling, not writing, will be the test here. I plan on doing future books with coauthors who really bring something to the page and really want to write. With the many others who approach me, I'm polite but say no thanks.

One of the most common problems with "helpers" is that they are in love with every little bit they contribute (which is not always great, or perfectly fitting for the subject or your style). If you don't use it, it's a real stab in the heart to them and your friendship. You can easily end up spending more energy and emotion tending them than the material at hand.

Then comes the pay part. People assume that you are really making money because you are a writer, so they don't say it, but they often expect some big financial return, or at least their name in lights.

Equal partnerships are good, but they are rare. Someone generally ends up carrying most of the burden, and your writing partner, whether 100 percent helpful or not, may stick to you like glue. So be careful, and if you do have doubts, don't get into it. Getting out is sticky because everything is "in writing" (no pun intended).

One more thing about being or feeling alone. Remember we always overestimate how well things are going for others and think we are "losing it" or missing some inspiration or intelligence when we hit a little slowdown in our projects. We see others as sailing through life, often unaware that they may have more problems and feel just as lonely as we do. So don't sweat the alone feeling once in a while in writing. It's healthy. If your book seems to be headed toward permanent hold, or you seem to be running on empty, then go out and select a helper. But fast and pray before you commit!

IF YOU DO DECIDE TO SEEK A COLLABORATOR OR GHOSTWRITER

Here are some lower-budget ways to find one close to home:

- Check with local newpapers to see if there is someone who covers (or is interested in) subjects like yours who might like to collaborate, or write the book for you.

- If there is a writers conference held nearby, attend it for a day, and seek out the people attending the sessions most related to your type of book. Look for one with decent credentials and/or a flair for the type of writing you need.

- Check with the writing programs at your local colleges to see if the professors there might recommend a talented student capable of the job.

The following are some channels more likely to lead you to an established pro (who is also likely to be more expensive):

- Look in the "Editorial Services" section of *Literary Market Place* (available at libraries) for people offering collaboration and ghostwriting aid.

- Ask a custom book producer such as The Jenkins Group (www.bookpublishing.com) or About Books, Inc. (www.About-books.com) to help you find a collaborator.

- If you've read a book similar to yours and liked the job the person did on it, find the author's (or his agent's) address and see if he would be interested. If the author has an agent, he will often be mentioned in the acknowledgments. *Literary Market Place* can then give you the phone number of that agency. If you write to an author c/o their publisher, the publisher will usually forward the letter on to the author.

- Get the directory of the American Society of Journalists and Authors (at this writing, it costs $98) and look through the detailed listings for writers who do your kind of book. Or consult the ASJA's writer referral service. Then you can call or write the candidates to see if they are interested in your project, and how much it would cost if they took it on.

CHAPTER 7

Putting
It All
Together

Your book box is ripe and ready. Now it's time to take your building materials and build your book. I really like this part, and I think you will, too.

It's totally your call now. You decide when and how you will put it all together. This is not hard, it just requires some concentration—a few good "sittings" with no interruptions.

The following is what works well for me.

RULE 1 My first rule is:

Alone, Quiet, and Room

Find a place that is quiet, where you can be alone, that has plenty of room (table or floor space) to lay things out.

There is really no way anyone can help you here. It is your book. You've put all that material into the box, and only you will know what you intended to do with it and what you want your book to say.

RULE 2

Then I scan the contents of my box quickly and divide my subject into the major subtopics I see within it (the chapters), and make a file folder for each of these chapters. I lay those folders out in order, in a fan shape. I may change the chapters or the order later, but I do it as I see it now.

RULE 3

Then I lay seven or eight blank pages at the base of each folder.

RULE 4

Now I set my box in the middle of the floor and start pulling out the notes, clippings, and pieces of writing. I put them with the chapter they seem to belong in. When everything has been sorted this way, I go through each chapter pile, trim off any excess paper, and tape the notes and clips neatly in a row on the blank sheets in no particular order. I am just getting the book's beginning, middle, and ending material roughly sorted out.

These taped-together pages are easy to read, to rip things off of, or to add to. When one page is full, I drop it in the folder it belongs in and start another page.

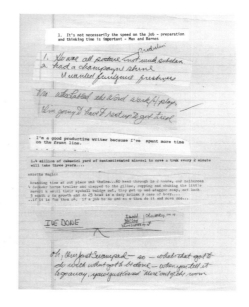

While you are doing this, chapter titles and additional chapters you may need will evolve by themselves.

You really need to stick with this initial sorting process—no visiting or breaks—because once you get in the flow of this, you'll amaze yourself with your speed and sorting skill. Plus you'll remember it all and retain it. Don't break the rhythm. Often I've sorted through an entire book in one fourteen-hour day.

If you do have to take a break or change locations now, you'll have all your folders set up and marked and some partly filled, and you can set it all out quickly again.

RULE 5   Once you have everything in the box divided up like this, you have a roughly organized book with some of your chapter titles and some headings within the chapters. Everything has been distributed into eight to fifteen or so file folders and you are fresh on what you have collected, no matter how long ago.

As you get to this point, all kinds of new ideas for your book will pop into your head. Just jot them down and toss them into their respective folders now that you have dismantled the old collection box. It's surprising how much you'll come up with while you are assembling your book. Just put it in the right file and add it in later.

A table of contents is the very first thing I do when writing a book. It's always my organizational skeleton. I generally end up changing the order a bit and improving the names of some of the chapters, but I get them down first.

RULE 6   Now you are at the point where you can actually begin to write the draft of the entire book on a typewriter, computer, or by hand. I open each folder, look at all my taped-on bits, untape them as necessary, move them around into a beginning-to-end order, and fill in around them or with them. Or I check them off and write up something from the idea.

I also like to put in art and design ideas as I go.

You will use most of your notes and "snippets" up now. If some don't fit, don't force them. Set those aside, and go on to the next file.

Sometimes, depending on the condition of this first rough, I take this assemblage of pasted-up and written pieces and have one of my staff members quickly enter it into a computer. This takes it from "cave man" to "carry around" stage so that it is clearer and neater and others can understand it.

Once I am to this point, I make a couple of extra copies of the rough chapters, just in case, and put one in a ring binder. I like to have a tangible, physical book that I can see. Being assured that it's on the computer or on a disk is not enough for me.

I carry the ring binder copy around with me and read, correct, fix, add to, and improve it. Then I have these changes made on the computer, which can be done in no time. At this point a pretty decent manuscript, maybe as far as you can take it right now, will be there.

Editing

By who? Why?

Your book won't be too effective yet after this rough drafting process and the first changes you've made. You know and love your work so much you cannot and will not see glaring problems. Now comes your first real experience—editing. I don't mean editing for grammar, punctuation, or that old English teacher stuff. I mean editing—having someone read it with a cold eye and tell you what is wrong or right and what it really needs to fly. You need someone (preferably a professional) to give you a reality check on your writing. Here, I believe, is a truly critical step for your book, finding someone with skill enough to see and honest enough to tell you the truth about your book so far.

After dreaming about and collecting for your book so long and writing so much, you'll be emotionally attached to every word and any slashing done will be as painful as if it were being done to your own body. But "cleaning up" a manuscript is an act of love, not an axing of your abilities. Look at this—the following page was written, typed, edited by three of us amateurs, printed, and sold 20,000 copies. Then editor Carol Cartaino zipped through my "perfect" book, and this is what I got back.

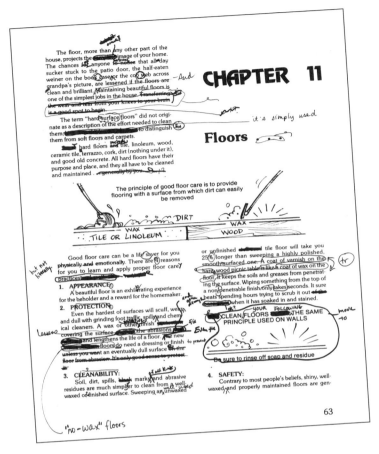

The harder you are edited (by the right person), the better you and your books get. Page 80 shows another page from the same book. One little section of my book was eliminated entirely. It was my masterpiece, I thought—I worked on it for two whole days and prayed and meditated over it, too. She had no mercy, but she was right. Not all drafts need this much editing, but they all need some.

The pages I've reproduced here show you many of the smaller changes an editor may make in your work. But the most important editing, as indicated earlier, is the overall feedback a good editor will give you to let you know if your book is in fact doing whatever you intended it to do. If your manuscript is meant purely as an entertainment, for instance, is it truly (and always) entertaining? If it is meant to explain how to do something, does it do so clearly and well? This kind of editing (called content editing) will tell you whether your book

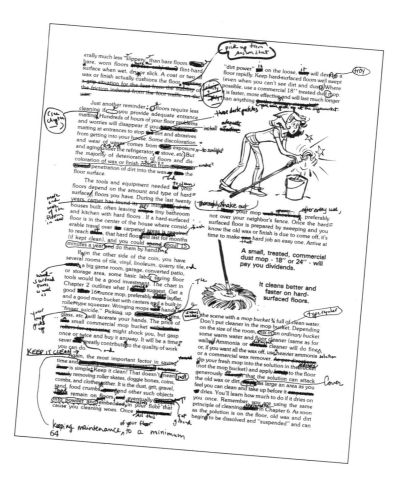

is satisfying in general, whether the parts of it are in the best possible order, and whether there are important things you left out (or things that *ought* to be left out!).

Where will you find an editor? Lots of publishers have pretty good editors, and they will work with you to improve your book if they are publishing it. If you're self-publishing, you need to find a "freelancer" (an independent editor for hire). You can find many listed in *Literary Market Place* (the official directory of the book business) under "Editorial Services."

If you have no choice but to edit yourself (this is hard, even for the real pros), do it after the manuscript is done and you've been away from it for at least a few days, not while you are still writing the book.

An editor will find the gaps and cut the chaff that you cannot see in your own work.

Expert readers

The expert reader is different. Especially if your book covers a technical, scientific, or specialized subject of any kind, it's usually a good idea to have someone else knowledgeable in the area read it while it is still in manuscript form. No matter how much you know about your subject, even if you are "the" expert in it, bar none, someone else in your field will see things you missed or need. You don't have to do everything they say, but their comments are always worth listening to.

Friends aren't usually good expert readers. They will fib and politic you. Get a good, mean expert reader, even a competitor. You'll both like each other a little better after the experience. Expert readers are often paid an "honorarium" for their trouble. This means they are paid something (say $50 or $100 or more), though not necessarily what their time is truly worth. If necessary or appropriate, you may pay them by the hour instead. Be sure to set a time limit here, or they'll delay the job forever because they're busy with other things. It's embarrassing to keep asking, "Are you done yet, Harry?"

> I'd rather have people love or hate my work than think it is "interesting." People who say "it's interesting" don't like it!

ILLUSTRATIONS

You have another book choice now—illustrations or not. How many? What kind? Who should do them? These are good questions, too. It's fun to decorate a book or create some graphics to help get your message across.

Often one good drawing, map, or picture can replace several pages of print explanation and direction. And illustrations and graphics give the reader a break. Most readers visualize heavily (put their own art in) as they read, but a little help in this department is a real asset to a book, especially these days.

If you publish your book with a publisher, it will have a part (maybe a big one) in deciding whether your book should be illustrated, and in what way.

Some authors spend a few hundred dollars for art in their book. I've spent $15,000 for my best book and an average of $7,000 for all of them. That tells you how important I consider art to be in a book. I feel it is almost mandatory. A lot of great authors got away (and still do) without one single illustration in their books. And their books are wonderful. In "the old days," readers didn't expect art in books, and a photo or sketch or two between the covers was savored, a special treat. Today we have a fast-paced and highly visual world. Anything that can grab attention and entertain will be picked over anything plain. We're conditioned to expect visuals now.

We can easily test this—what catches your eye and coaxes you to buy or read things?

Chapter 3
Housebreaking
The #1 Solution the #1 Pet Cleaning Problem

f thorough housebreak-
emphasized. Everything
rthwhile, enjoyable
royed if htey can't be
se. —The American

round it—housetraining
your whole relationship
e dogs are abandoned
problems than for any
ll talk about house-
the equally important
ats is covered later

erful forces on our
reaking process. Dogs
because their natural
t in with our house
never want to soil
re they sleep or eat—
ld puppy will stumble
o urinate.

CHAPTER **3.**

House-breaking

The #1 Solution to the #1 Pet Cleaning Problem

The importance of thorough housebreaking cannot be overemphasized. Everything that makes dogs worthwhile, enjoyable companions is destroyed if they can't be trusted in the house.
—The American Kennel Club

There's no way around it—house-training can make or break your whole relationship with your pet. More dogs are abandoned for house-soiling problems than for any other reason. (We'll talk about housebreaking dogs here; the equally important house-training of cats is covered later in the chapter.)

We have some powerful forces on our side in the housebreaking process. Dogs are easy to train because their natural instincts fit right in with our house environment. Dogs never want to soil their den—foul where they sleep or eat—even a four-week-old puppy will stumble away from his box to urinate.

Where does art come from?

Mostly from YOU. "But I can't draw!"

Well, neither can I. My books often have hundreds of pieces of art in them, and about a third of those illustration ideas are mine. I originate lots of that artwork in the rough while I am writing using good old "stick people."

Probably only about 1 percent of authors do their own final artwork, so don't get uptight here. I'd love to be an artist and a musician, too, but drawing stick people and putting a good CD in the player seem to be my limit.

All you have to do as you're working on your book is collect pictures, layouts, and art styles that you see and like, and think might benefit your book. And make little rough sketches, or just notes, wherever you see a place in your manuscript that really cries out to be illustrated.

> I love making rough layouts, charts, and stick people as I write or read my drafts—I have a kind of "sketch it out as I see it" approach. This violates the usual procedure of carefully separating text and artwork in the draft, but it works well for me. We are all artists at heart (or in our next life), and here is a chance to express it.

Find a real artist now

When it comes to converting your roughs into finished art, remember that readers are used to good art these days. Once the word is out that you're doing a book, you may have all kinds of "artists" contacting you with an eye to doing your artwork, including relatives. Artists are easy to find; good ones are less common. If you intend to have art in your book, make sure you get one of those good ones. In the long run, I've found that the most expensive one is often the cheapest—they are faster and smarter, and their work really enhances your writing.

When I have an artist in mind, I send him some of my draft manuscript along with my stick art ideas and a letter like the following:

MARSH CREEK PRESS
A division of Don Aslett Inc.

January 1, 2005

Art Inkletter
114 Scenic Terrace
Paint Valley, AZ 12345

RE: Request for Art Sample / Bid

Dear Art:

I am looking for an illustrator for my new book titled CATS AND ALL THEY DRAG IN, and you were recommended to me by my friends at Primecats Press. My book will need 30-40 illustrations and will be published in spring of next year.

Enclosed are two sample pages from this book that need to be illustrated and my own roughs of an art idea for each of these. I have also enclosed some photocopied pages from my other books to show you the kind of illustrations my books usually have.

Could you send me a couple of rough preliminary sketches in the style you think would be suited to this book?

After I have your sample sketches, I will give you a call to discuss them, and hopefully to visit with you in detail on the number and type of illustrations, fees, and schedule.

Sincerely,

Don Aslett

PO BOX 700
POCATELLO
IDAHO 83204

311 S FIFTH AVE
POCATELLO
IDAHO 83201

PH 208-232-3535
FX 208-235-5481

Don't let this "art" thing scare or discourage you. Good artists know what they are worth (this is one way you can distinguish between the pros and the amateurs). But most artists will charge less per illustration when they get to illustrate an entire book. A lot depends too, as with all people with services for hire, on how much other work they have right now and how eager they are to do the job. You might be able to trade something for the work or get the whole book done for a deal. A good artist's work for my *Clean in a Minute* cost book $1,500 for everything. That little book has made me over $70,000 in profit.

I keep a file on every artist who approaches me, and I keep looking for talented new ones. Judith Holmes Clarke of California, a former Disney artist, made my first two books memorable ones. John Caldwell, in New York, does illustrations for *MAD* magazine and *Writer's Digest,* among others. He blew me away with his art for *The Office Clutter Cure*—his ideas and illustrations were phenomenal. I've never met him. David Locke, of England, has illustrated five of my books with impish, understated charm. I finally met him on a trip there.

Art by Judith Holmes Clarke

Art by
Judith Holmes Clarke

Art by John Caldwell

I lost a talented young artist, Robert L. Betty, to diabetes. His art was always exuberantly alive, and his cartoon animals were unequaled. Kerry Otteson, another Idahoan, helped bring many of my publications, large and small, to life.

Art by Robert L. Betty

Art by Kerry Otteson

A versatile artist I use often is Craig LaGory of Cincinnati. Not only can he do both cartoon and "straight technical" art, but he is also a designer. This makes it easier to come up with a layout and total "package" that really fits a book, both the text and the art. From Craig I can get a cover, book design, and artwork. And best of all, he loves his profession—he gets excited about what he's doing and really takes part in the book, which make the whole process a pleasure. Craig did the artwork for this book.

Art by Craig LaGory

Illustrating a book is exciting. There are no rules or boundaries, and you and your illustrator can come up with things that no one, even the greatest artists, ever has before.

Many books can be attractively illustrated with "scene setting" or "mood creating" line illustrations, such as the following two illustrations by Jack Homesley and R. Bruce Laughlin in Patricia Penton Leimbach's books on farm life.

Other books and subjects need more precise and "technical" illustrations, such as the one below, and the "home cleaning closet" on page 92.

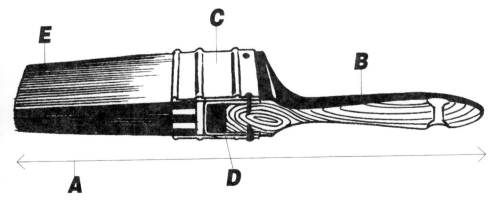

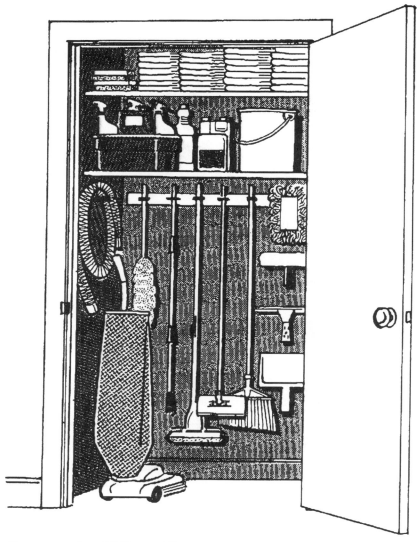

How much will it cost?

Here are ballpark costs for illustrating the average book, from Craig LaGory. As of 2002, he charges $50 an hour.

Black and white line art (most book illustration is done in black and white to keep printing costs down): Most quarter- to half-page illustrations (cartoons, technical illustrations, or sketches meant to decorate or create a mood) can be done for $50* each unless they're highly technical.

Most full-page illustrations will range from $50* to $250* each.

Black and white airbrush art: Quarter- to half-page illustrations: $50–$100.* Full page illustrations: $100–$200*.

Color art: Quarter- to half-page illustrations: $50–$250.* Full page illustrations: $100–$400*.

Cover designs and art: Design: $400 (includes two black-and-white roughs and one color rough). Finished art: $100–$1000, depending on complexity.

* Includes the initial idea and one rough for an illustration. There will be additional charges if more ideas or many revisions are required.

(You can call Craig for a free estimate for illustrating your own book, at 513-271-4818.)

Most artists can illustrate the average book (one hundred illustrations or less) in about a month. To keep costs down—and help avoid errors and aggravation—you want to make changes and corrections to the illustrations when they start (as soon as you see the roughs), not after they finish.

A good illustrator will not just make a picture of what you already said—he or she will dramatize it, add a dimension to it, to help bring it home to the reader.

An illustration from my Stainbuster's Bible.

To Bleach
or Not to Bleach

Make it legal!

Once you've decided on an artist, to avoid misunderstandings and problems, be sure to draw up a written agreement with him. It doesn't have to be complicated, but it should specify how many illustrations of what kind he will do for what price, in what time period, and what rights you have to these illustrations. (Can you use them forever, in all domestic and foreign editions, and on cocktail napkins, magazine articles, and posters too, or what?) Also make clear who will have the copyright on the illustrations. When I pay for art, I want to own it.

Unless you are a super salesperson, you, not the publisher, will be paying for the art in your book. I think this is wrong, but trying to change a publisher's established way of doing things takes more energy than writing ten books! I loved working with Writer's Digest, and it was willing to share the cost of the artwork on some of our projects together.

If it does pay for any art, the publisher will probably assume ownership of it and hold the copyright on it.

Clip art—the low-priced alternative!

If your book needs illustrations, or even just visual relief, and you can't afford to hire an illustrator, clip art is one good answer. Clip art is readily available from software companies and catalogs. And it's cheap! There are thousands of art styles to choose from and all kinds of images.

The trick is to find illustrations that match, or better yet, enhance what you're saying in your manuscript. The downfall of clip art, besides that it probably won't perfectly portray your copy because it has to be generic by its very nature, is that an illustrated book should look all of a piece. Using illustrations by one artist here and another there, one style of clip art here and another there, totally defeats the purpose of book design, which is to make a book inviting and easy to read so the reader doesn't even notice what goes into it. When two elements clash, like different styles of clip art, it "stops" the reader—he may not know why or what is wrong, but it interrupts him nevertheless.

I put out a book on poetry writing quickly one year to use as a Christmas present for family and friends. We used clip art for speed, and because of the varied nature and subject matter of the poems, it worked out fine.

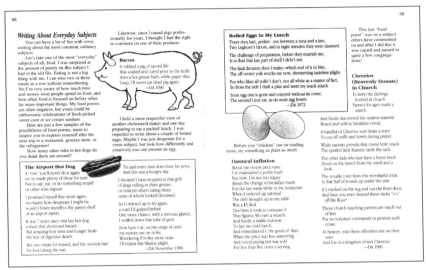

Clip art is an inexpensive way to lend some drama to a book, as these pages from my book on writing poetry show.

PHOTOS

Again remember that today, good photos are everywhere, and people expect quality photos. Fuzzy, cluttered, or mismatched pictures tossed onto a page aren't going to cut it. You're better off having no photos at all than bad ones. You can occasionally get by with "freebie" illustrations such as those from manufacturers' publicity departments or government agencies, or Photostatted from library collections, depending on your subject. But here, too, quality is important. Just because it's free or cheap doesn't mean you should use it. The question is, does it do what you want and need the picture in that spot to do?

If you take a photo for your book and it doesn't fit and you don't like it, redo it. Take another quick trip to the site and take some more pictures, or have more taken. Film is inexpensive, and books are forever, so it's always good to have a selection to choose from. Once *People* magazine took more than 1,200 pictures of me for an article, didn't get what it wanted, and flew me to New York and took two hundred more. And used **three**. But the ones it used were just right. I know you and I don't have a budget like that, but there may be a reason *People* sells millions of copies!

If your photos contain people, make sure anyone pictured signs a release. If you have children, you can use them for models and you don't have to pay them or get releases.

And be sure to take out copyright on your photos if you've taken them yourself.

If you can't take good pictures yourself and don't have a spouse, friend, or grown child who can, then consider hiring a professional photographer. Look for one who does the type of photos you need—action shots, pictures of objects (such as nicely posed collectibles), scenic natural views, or underwater photos, for example.

Often nothing can illustrate what you want or need to illustrate better than a photograph.

Black-and-white photos are much less expensive to print than color (see chapter ten). Photos can either be put in "inserts" (the little photo albums we see stuck here and there in biographies and the like), or scattered through the book. Ideally there should be some kind of uniformity in your use of photos, such as photos only at chapter openings, or several photos per chapter.

"With photographs, accept the fact that the number of photos and illustrations will change, from the day you first make the list to the very last stage of the book, for many reasons you can't predict. Some you'll decide you don't need, some will not be usable for permission reasons, some will seem to duplicate others, etc. So be sure to come up with a numbering system that you can carry through to the end, and add to and subtract from with a minimum of confusion. Make the system as simple as possible. If you use an arbitrary system, you'll end up with chaos for sure.

When you send in photos to a publisher, be sure to identify them on the back with the heading in the book, and the manuscript page, where they belong. This will help assure that all photos end up in the right place."

—*DR. JEAN LOFTUS,*
author and plastic surgeon

CHAPTER 8

THE BIG CHOICE NOW:
FIND A PUBLISHER,
OR SELF-PUBLISH?

"…writing is never completed until it's published… Something written in a so-called ivory tower for oneself alone, to be shared with no one else, is not completed writing, and those who believe that it is are deluding themselves…"
—*JAMES A. MICHENER*

Okay, I've got my book manuscript and illustrations—NOW WHAT?

Now comes the fun part, and a big choice. And both of these options are positive. You can

1. Self-publish—Take your book all the rest of the way yourself, even printing it yourself, and own it 100 percent.

2. Use a publisher—There are thousands of publishers out there who make a living taking authors' manuscripts (like yours), producing books from them, and then distributing them, paying all the expenses of this and paying a royalty to the author on copies sold.

Let me take you briefly through my own self-publishing experience because like you, I had a first book.

While in college, I started a cleaning business of my own, Varsity Contractors, to pay for my schooling and support myself and my young family. As I progressed through school, both my family and my business grew. Soon I was an expert in the cleaning field and had a company that was operating in three states, as I worked eighteen-hour days to fit in both school and work, plus the many community activities I was involved in. When I finished college, I taught high school for a couple of years, but my cleaning business just kept on growing and soon demanded my full-time attention.

I kept records, notes, and files on cleaning all the while and was soon doing lectures and classes for church groups, PTAs, women's clubs, extension classes, schools, and anyone who asked. Although cleaning is a dull and dreaded chore, I was in demand because everyone has to do it, and I promised to teach them how to do it faster yet better. The more I taught this, the more humor and visual aids I developed to help get it across, and the bigger the crowds got. First twenty, then sixty, then a hundred people, then two or three hundred. It was fun, because changing lives for the better—on the stage or on the page—is a thoroughly rewarding pastime.

With all of these lectures and classes came a lot of questions from the audiences: How this and why that and when should and what do you use? All of this told me one thing as clear as a newly cleaned window—people wanted to know more.

I decided to do a small handout just to answer the most common questions: about walls, toilets, rugs, floors, windows, and bathrooms. While working on a big cleaning job in California, I had a little time left over, so I sat in a hotel room one afternoon and wrote up a twelve-page brochure titled "The Adventures of Betty Betterhouse" (I didn't know a thing about sexism in those days). I handed it to a young mother who did some art on the side, and she drew my stick men and women up into a little more recognizable species. Then I printed up about a thousand of my little booklets and priced them at one dollar. I printed them for a dime each, so that was a 10x markup. I took them with me to my next seminar, held in a high school auditorium. It seated 600, and it was full. I did my dashing cleaning demos, leaping around and laughing and slinging suds and showing them how the pros did it. I promised them that they could do the same in their homes and cut their cleaning time up to 75 percent. When I finished, I laid the "books" (brochures, really) out on the edge of the stage and told people that if they wanted to know more, there was a little book available for just a dollar. They could come up and take one and toss a buck in the box. As soon as my presentation was over, it was like a shark feeding frenzy. Women pushed and shoved, kicked and cussed (church women, too) to get their copy of the "little book." Have you ever seen $600 in a pile of one-dollar bills? I thought I'd gone to janitor's heaven. I scooped up my first profits from a happy crowd, and as I drove home, I said to myself out loud: "I'm going to do a book on how to clean."

Keenly motivated after seeing the demand for information, I began the next day, in my spare time (I was running a large contracting business, remember, had six kids, and was really busy, just like you are right now). Since I'd been collecting all kinds of cleaning information for some time, in a couple of months of part-time work I had the book basically done with my old Olympia typewriter and a yellow pad. There is something about having your first book finished (at least I thought it was finished) that makes you feel powerful and arrogant, so I let my best friend, Mark Browning, one of my managers with a brilliant mind, read it. He was too honest to be nice and was pretty critical about the attitude he saw in there, the tone it was written in: kind of like, "This is the only right way to do it, and if you don't clean like this, you're dumb!"

I was taken aback that there could possibly be anything wrong with the book, but respecting his wisdom and knowing inside that he was right, I removed some of the moralizing and criticism. Then I had my secretary type up the semi-finished manuscript. It looked so clean and neat and beautiful to me—I was right where you will be at that point with your book. Now I had a manuscript in hand, and what was I supposed to do with it? I asked and was told what I told you—you can do it yourself or have a publisher publish it. I was plenty busy with my business and "publisher" sounded so big and full of authority that going through a publisher was what I decided to do.

I made about ten copies of the manuscript, got myself a *Writer's Market* (see the Resource List in the back of this book), copied the names and addresses of some of the most impressive publishers, and sent off my book. I was inexperienced and idealistic enough that I fully expected to hear back within a few days, not longer than a week, from all ten fighting to get the rights to my masterpiece. But there was nothing… nothing… for two weeks, nothing for four weeks, and then finally after ten weeks I got a noncommittal reply from one saying that they "couldn't include it in their list at this time." Eventually I got all my manuscripts, or most of them, back with the same kind of note. Not one had even a sentence of encouragement.

This, folks, is reality when it comes to book publishers as I learned again years later working with the world's biggest and best publishers in New York. One editor (at one of the publishers of Ian Fleming's famous "James Bond" series) said she got about fifty manuscripts a day, and one day she got two hundred. Other editors told me the same things, that their offices were full of manuscripts and they were months behind in reading them—and here comes another big bunch in the mail. Yet there are all of those anxious writers out there sending off their heart and soul in one package. The truth is that most of those manuscripts are never read, just

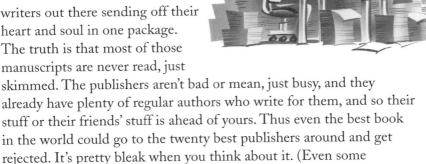

skimmed. The publishers aren't bad or mean, just busy, and they already have plenty of regular authors who write for them, and so their stuff or their friends' stuff is ahead of yours. Thus even the best book in the world could go to the twenty best publishers around and get rejected. It's pretty bleak when you think about it. (Even some bestsellers like *Gone with the Wind* and *Chicken Soup for the Soul* were rejected many times by publishers.)

Publishers often have rigid criteria for what they publish, and a dozen brilliant books a day could (and do) go right past them. Then they will advance $3 million to some dim-witted adulterer for his "book." It doesn't make sense, but that's the way it is in publishing, and that's why I self-publish now.

So what am I saying? Just this—getting your book really looked at and read is more difficult than just mailing it to a publisher. Even I, after selling more than two million books, sent off six nice books to publishers a few years ago, and only two publishers wanted to visit on them. This is just a warning that even if you pick publishing through a big house, it doesn't mean that they will pick you.

What about agents? Getting an agent to represent your first book isn't necessarily the answer considering that it's almost as hard to get an agent as a publisher and the agent will take a good-size chunk of your earnings if the book does sell. It's much easier to get an agent after you have some success in the book world under your belt. If you want to try to get one now, some of the books listed in the Resource List will tell you how.

In my own case, I guess I had enough self-confidence and feedback from my cleaning seminars that I knew my book, once out, would sell. So I went to visit a prominent local publisher in a nearby big city (I'd sent him a book previously). He sat there cocksure behind his big desk and informed me that cleaning would not sell, that everyone hated it, and that my cutesy approach (that's what he called my cartoons and humor) would never work. My book, if it ever would have a chance, would have to be serious and solid, factual how-to.

The publisher route wasn't working, so on to Plan B—publish it myself. I didn't have a clue as to how to do that. I got my wife and teenage daughter to do a final typed version of the manuscript. I'd met an artist, Judith Holmes Clarke, in California while doing a seminar, and I had her do some humorous art for the book. I found a part-time photographer to take a picture of a cartoon character on a new broom against a gingham background for the cover. At another seminar my friend Gladys Allen came up with a great title, *Is There Life After Housework?* I had a great gag chapter in the book—chapter four, "What to Expect Out of Husbands and Children." It was nothing but four blank pages with some dirty smudges on them. It was funny, and in fact the whole book, factual as it was, was funny.

I took the finished manuscript down to a printer in Salt Lake City, and the employees there shook their heads a bit at my some of my ideas and illustrations and my farm-boy style, but they were helpful.

"How many books do you want?" they asked. I always think big, and since the printer offered a price break for 20,000 copies, I said 20,000. I scraped together the money to print these books in pure faith, bad judgment, or total ignorance. I had them delivered to my house, not the office, because I had "some room" in the garage. Gadfrey—have you ever seen 20,000 8.5 x 11 books? They brought them in a tractor-trailer, and there wasn't room for the car for a long time afterward.

In my innocence I was sure that I would unload all these books quickly—and I did—in just six months, they were gone. They cost $1.30 to print, and I sold them for $5, so I made around $60,000 on this project. I knew my market, and I was right—homemakers wanted information on cleaning. I sold these books mainly at my seminars and by mail, no bookstores.

On to the Olympics of bookselling!

At this point I learned that there was an actual convention of bookbuyers and sellers called the ABA (American Booksellers Convention). It would be held in Chicago this year, and just about every publisher in the country would be there. This sounded like the place to be, so my wife and I took thirty cases of books (we only needed one case, as it turned out, because this was a place to show books and take orders for them, not actually sell them). I remember my luggage stopped the United Airlines conveyor belt, it was so heavy.

We also knew nothing about booths at an exposition like this. We found a bargain booth at the last minute for $250. Little did we know that the bigger and better booths were $5,000 and $10,000 and that ours was around the corner, behind the pillars and across the forklift tracks next to the restrooms. So we showed up to peddle our single book using a smaller version of the cover for our decorations. Others had fifty, a hundred, two hundred, or more new books in huge lighted displays and Jane Fonda, the Incredible Hulk, and Richard Simmons there in person to call attention to them.

But we did have a book that would sell

In the next three days, I met scores of publishers and other authors in person, got acquainted with many of them, and had a taste of "book society." I was not overimpressed—it was maybe a notch above Hollywood—but there was lots of big talk and strutting around. Fortunately for me, a few people had to go to the bathroom and thus right by our booth. Two or three of them actually stopped. First was an editor from the *National Enquirer* who paged through my book and then laid it down and said, "You have a bestseller there, son. We don't do books, but I tell you that will sell!" Then a trim, athletic-looking man in a neat suit stopped, looked at my book, and asked if he might take two copies back to his office. He introduced himself as Budge Wallis, CEO of Writer's Digest Books, a well-known publisher of books for writers. I gave him the books, and the rest of the show was a "wow" education about the book business. I recommend you attend one (these gatherings are called BookExpo America now, and you can find out about them at http://bookexpo.reedexpo). A few bookstore people stopped by, but we didn't sell one book, so we lugged those thirty cases back home.

While I was getting my initiation into the book business, my cleaning company was gaining ground with one of our biggest clients, The Bell System. Two years before, I'd helped design (as a consultant on the cleaning and maintenance aspects) a big new 3 million-square-foot building for them in Atlanta. Now we'd been awarded the cleaning contract on the building and so were expanding into Georgia. I was in Atlanta one afternoon and was paged out of a meeting for a call from Writer's Digest. It was Budge Wallis, and he said, "We like your book and would like to publish it. We will edit, redesign, reprint, and distribute it. We will put you on tour and on TV and pay you ten percent of the cover cost (about a dollar a book) for royalties."

I had cleaning seminars set up all over, new buildings under way, and my company just kept on growing. I didn't have much time to try to push my book into the big leagues myself, and I didn't know anything about it, either. So I said, "Yes, Mr. Wallis, you can have it." Later I learned that several of the critics and advisers there had looked my book over, chuckled over it, and tucked it into the reject pile. But the head editor, Carol Cartaino, read it thoughtfully. "This guy has some rough edges," she reported to the committee that decides the fates of submissions, " but he does know his stuff, and this book will sell. It's a truly different approach to cleaning."

So they went on to publish it, a small but great publishing company in Cincinnati. The book went on the bestseller list, and for ten lovely days I was ahead of *The Joy of Sex* and *30 Days to a Beautiful Bottom*. After the book took off, Cartaino in her wisdom (here is another important job of an editor) called and said, "Can you write us another book?" "Two books on cleaning?" I whined. "Yes," she said. (Since then I've done more than a dozen on cleaning and have more in the hopper. Even the mundane job of cleaning has many angles.)

She suggested a question-and-answer book, and that was all I needed. People did ask me cleaning questions hourly, so before long we'd assembled one hundred questions about cleaning into *Do I Dust or Vacuum First?* It coattailed on Life After Housework and was on the bestseller list too, and went on to sell more than 350,000 copies. I'd found a great publisher, and they a profitable author. They did my next four books, and my sales were good.

By the time I had my next crop of books ready, Writer's Digest was concentrating more than ever on books for aspiring writers and then artists and other budding creatives, so we went to the "big leagues" and put my new books out for bid to all of the big publishers. It was pretty stimulating to see a dozen of the biggest and best all vying to get my books when ten years earlier they wouldn't even open the manuscript envelope. We had a full-scale book auction and ended up signing contracts to do three books for New American Library, a giant of the industry, and a cleaning encyclopedia for Dell. Later I did another for Simon & Schuster.

To summarize a long and not entirely profitable or productive experience, after completing those five books we concluded that from now on we could and would produce all of our own books. We had the best editor in the country, Carol Cartaino, great artists, and the same machines the publishers had. And so I completed the circle from successful self-publisher, to an author for publishers, then larger publishers, and then back to self-publishing. I like to own and control my own things, and I have the resources of people and money to do it. I can, and you can too, produce just as good a book as the "big boys" can. And you can and will pay more attention to your own book than a giant publisher will.

The big, often determining, factor for success here is distribution. How are you going to SELL your book? I travel all over and am experienced with the media, and still I struggle to sell some of my self-published books. Working through distributors like Ingram and Baker & Taylor is pretty cumbersome for us little guys. So if you go it yourself, expect to work for what you sell. If you don't like to market and sell, you probably shouldn't self-publish.

When you are published...

It's pretty cut and dried. A publisher takes your book and pays most of the expenses of producing it. They are gambling that it will make them money, and so they do it all after the book is written and thus have some incentive to push your book. They will give you a few free copies when the book first rolls off the press, but after that you have to buy your own books from them, generally at a 40 or 50 percent discount, unless you are buying in large quantities.

A publisher will put your book in its catalog and promote it, often along with hundreds of others. It will also try to market the other rights to it—see chapter nine. If your book sells, the publisher will pay more attention to it and push it harder. The bottom line is, the better it sells, the harder the publisher will work to sell it. That's how it makes money.

Publishers generally need to sell at least 10,000 copies to make money. 15,000 is better, over 20,000 is good, and 30,000 is getting into the gravy. Few books make it this high. For a paperback book you'll most likely get 6 percent royalties, maybe 8 percent, up to as high as 10 percent, usually in some kind of "escalations" or steps keyed to the number of copies sold. If your book is a proven seller, you might be able to get them to start right out at 10 percent. Hardcover books have a higher royalty, usually 10 percent going to 12.5 percent and then 15, again, in stages.

So you'll probably make $10,000–$15,000 or more if your book does well. Most authors make less than this on their books, or so the "big boys" and the other authors I know tell me. If your book lasts through the short six-month bookstore shelf life many books have today and keeps selling, the publisher will keep it on its "backlist" (see the Glossary). If it doesn't sell, the publisher will dump it, slowly or quickly, and someday give it back to you.

When you self-publish...

You do it all and pay it all and own it all, and if anything good or bad happens to your book, you are responsible for it. After such great success with publishers, why would I want to publish my own books? That's an easy answer. Paperbacks can cost as little as a dollar a copy to produce. When that book sells in the bookstore for $10, the printer gets a buck, you get (on a list price royalty) one dollar, and the other eight go to the publisher, the bookstore, and other middlemen such as wholesalers and distributors. When I publish this book with a publisher and get a 50 percent discount on the copies I buy, I have $5 plus shipping (say $1.30 postage and $.50 packaging) in a copy of the book. That means a $3.20 profit when I sell it at full retail.

When I publish the same book myself and have only a dollar's worth of out-of-pocket costs in it (such as when it is an older book that has earned out all of the non-printing expenses involved in producing it), I have a $9 margin to work with. I can discount it any way I like and make a lot more per copy. And I can put a catalog of all my books in the back of every book to generate more orders. I've gone out to seminars, speaking engagements, and home shows and sold $2,000 worth of books. If these are my own books, I come home with an $1,800 profit; if a publisher published them, that's more like $900.

And when you publish your own book, **you** control the whole process—pick the cover, trim size, page count, illustrations, the title, and how much and what kind of editing and publicity there will be.

Again, today is different than even ten years ago in the book business. You can do anything a publisher can do when it comes to putting out a good book. Modern computers and all of their amazing programs have simplified all the stages of book production and put the process in the hands of the common man. The distribution, as noted earlier, is the big question. How will you get your book out to the world, to buyers and readers?

If you speak and teach, I'd advise you to do your own books. You'll save a lot of headaches, have a fat profit spread, and own all the rights. And once you have the actual book out and selling, a big publisher may see it and grab it and make you a heck of a deal. You could have the best of both worlds.

This is knife sticking, but I've got to tell you. When my first book hit the big time and profits were rolling in and sales hit the two million mark, I took a copy of the sales figures and pasted them on the reject letter from that puffed-up local publisher (who said cleaning would never sell, or humor, either) and sent it back to him. He deserved it! Since receiving his sage advice, I've gone on to do thousands of humorous appearances on cleaning on radio and TV.

Whether you self-publish or are published, the printer in either case is just the mechanic—too many new writers seem to think that printing a book is publishing it.

Some in-between options

If you put out your own book and it sells well, you can send a copy of your book along with its sales history to publishers, and that will say more to them than the most beautifully written proposal or manuscript. There is a good chance that a publisher will publish or distribute it now since you have done the "test marketing" for them.

I self-publish my own books now, and a publisher buys my books from me and distributes them. This is sort of an in-between option in which I agree to absorb all the costs of editing, producing the book, and publicizing it, and the publisher buys it from me at about a 65 percent discount and carries it in its catalog and sells it to bookstores and specialty stores. The publisher also handles many of the subsidiary rights (see chapter nine).

You can also let a publisher publish your book and buy the printing materials from them at a nominal cost after the book has had a hopefully long life and then gone out of print. You can then reissue it yourself to give it a second life. I've done this with a number of my books, as have many other authors.

There are lots of options if your book is good.

"When my third book went out of print, my husband and I decided to print and distribute future copies ourselves. This was fairly easy because the book was already a finished product; we just got the plates, made a few small corrections and changes, and reprinted it.

I sell the book at my seminars and by mail order, through my other books."

—*DENIECE SCHOFIELD,*
homemaker and author

Money, money, money... (tackling the tacky!)

True, creative folks like us don't like to talk or even think much about money. We are in this for the glory and nobility of it all (except we will accept handsome royalties or cash for our labors!). But idealistic as we may be, money does enter into the book equation in a fairly big way. I have some off-the-wall opinions about books and money, and I'm not trying to convert you to my way of doing business, only to alert you to the possibilities of it all.

When I first started turning out books, I had income from other sources, as you probably do, so I didn't have to depend on my pen to put food on the table or pay the oil bill. Writing a book doesn't cost much if you do it right. There are topics that require some serious research, elaborate illustrations, or extensive travel, and this might require a sizable pool of money. But for books about kids, life, your business, food, faith, or animals, for example, the ideas are free. Collecting them and putting them together, doesn't cost much. If you pick a topic you love, you'll be willing to put in the time and can squeeze it in when you wouldn't have been doing much else, anyway. Then if a publisher picks it up, you can put out a book without breaking your piggybank.

Many people have an exaggerated idea about "advances" for books, money you get from the publisher before your book is done. Advances for ideas and promises can be risky for both the giver and the taker. Advance money is not free money. It is your own money, and you are simply borrowing it against your book, or taking out a loan on it. It has to be paid back out of your royalties.

You hear about celebrities and well-known writers getting advances of hundreds of thousands or more, but those are few indeed. The average advance on an average first book is somewhere between $3,000 and $10,000, and often that is all the book makes. It's amazing how smart those publishers are. The majority of advances are almost right on target with what the book sells (in fact, publishers compute the advance by calculating how much the book is likely to earn in its first year of sales and offering that amount to the author). A lot of authors get a nice advance, blow it (thinking their ship has finally come in), and then wait for the money on the book to come through. Well, the first year's money goes to repay the advance, and then the book dies and the author has gotten all he's going to get.

Personally, I don't like advances. They do guarantee that the publisher will get serious and get the book out, but I like trust better and to be paid for the merits and actual performance of the book, not hopes and expectations. I've had advances from publishers of as much as $150,000, and at times I've wished I hadn't any. They can give you a false sense of security and cloud your judgment.

On the other hand, since people in the know report that "nine out of ten books never earn out their advance," it might be a good idea to take that advance (since publishers rarely or never try to get an unearned advance back). The advance might be all you ever see for all of your work and effort.

It's your call!

IF YOU WANT TO SELF-PUBLISH, HOW MUCH MONEY WILL YOU NEED?

Much depends on the size and type of book you have (including whether it has illustrations, how deluxe a printing job it has to have, how much of it all you can do yourself, and how much you need help with, for example). But you will probably need between $10,000 and $20,000 to publish your own book and have it look and read as good as a book produced by a good publisher. If you use one of the less expensive routes described on pages 123–124 (as I did with my poetry book), you may be able to end up with a book in your hands for a total cost under $5,000.

Don't overspend—find a way with what you have

Whatever route you take, don't overspend on your book. Save your money. Don't borrow to do books, even from relatives.

And don't count on someone else to finance your book. If you have a good story, a good cause, and a real passion to do something about it—do it. If you wait around for grants or subsidies, help in writing and producing something, you're likely to wait forever. Do what you want to do on your own budget—you can. Writing is an inexpensive thing to do. You need very little money to come up with something polished and good. I do this—I work fourteen and sixteen hours a day to support my writing addiction. Don't let dreams of outside financing delay your desire to get your message out. Find a way!

You have all it takes to put out a good book—the enthusiasm, a great story or truth, and an audience that needs it. This is what you need most for a successful book. You need to go at this like I do— FIND A WAY WITH WHAT YOU HAVE.

Taxes

While we're talking about money, there is one more bottom-line benefit of doing a book. When you can show income from the under-taking, or at least a genuine effort to make a profit from it, you can deduct related travel, entertainment, research, reference books, any help you hire, even possibly the part of your home you use for your book writing enterprise. Anything you can show as a bona fide expense of your writing and publishing activities can save you money in taxes. Acquaint your accountant with your writing operation, and she'll show you all you need to know.

> Smart gamblers in Vegas and elsewhere are now documenting the money they have when they get there, so that if they win $20,000 at the tables they can show it took them $10,000 to do it. Writers need to be that smart. However, remember that writing isn't gambling. Writing will **always** pay off in the end if you persist!

——— Being published vs. self-publishing, at a glance ———

Prestige in the eyes of the public	Your book will be respected if it sells
Publisher provides helpers, such as editors and designers	You may need to hire others to help
Publisher pays to produce and market your book	You pay the cost of producing and marketing it
You will get royalties only	If the book succeeds, you will get a larger share of the profits
If the book fails, you will lose only your time and energy (which will have been at least partially subsidized by the advance, if there was one)	If the book fails, you will lose both your time and the production costs of the book
Publisher will have control of the title, cover, size, price, and contents of the book	You get to decide all this
The publisher will schedule and direct all of the operations on your book, including the writing	You will make the schedule and direct all of the operations on your book
The publisher will promote and publicize your book to some extent, and you will do all you can to assist and enhance those efforts	You will plan and do all of the promotion and publicity for your book
The publisher will decide how to sell your book and do it, hopefully with some energy, though there is no guarantee of that	You will decide how to sell your book and do everything necessary to do so
The publisher will share in the profits of the subsidiary rights and make at least some effort to sell them	You will have complete ownership of all subsidiary rights but also have to find a way to exercise them
Your book will be one among many being published by the publisher, and it may get a decent amount of attention, or not	You love your book, so you will go all out for it
Entire process is slow and ponderous	You can move quickly
Your book must be accepted by a publisher, often a long and discouraging process	You can decide to put your book in print, and no one can stop you

CHAPTER 9

If You Want to Find a Publisher

Let's get this down to the basics:

1. There are thousands of publishers out there, and they are hungry for good books.
2. They want (and need!) to make money on books.
3. But you have to approach them, unless you are famous or luck into a publisher seeking an expert in your field.
4. Little or big publisher? Either works, and both have advantages and disadvantages. Any experience with either will be valuable to your career. Making sure your subject is their specialty, or one they know how to sell, is the key.

When you approach a publisher:

1. Select one up front that does the type of book you have, or have in mind. Getting a copy of one of the market guides listed in the Resource List, absorbing it, and really acting on it will save you much time and money, and many rejection slips. After you spend a few evenings here, you will know what to do, I promise you!

2. You need to help publishers see your book as a business opportunity and give them evidence of this, not just come begging.

3. Send a query letter (see the Glossary) ahead telling them about your book and that it is coming—would they like to see it? This should be one to three pages describing and outlining your book in as compelling a way as possible. You can also do the longer form of advance sales document known as a proposal. *Writer's Market, How to Write Irresistible Queries, How to Write a Book Proposal, Formatting and Submitting Your Manuacript,* and many other books published by Writer's Digest can give you every detail of how to put your best foot forward here.

In your query or proposal, be sure to include something powerful about yourself—remember, they are buying more than a stack of paper in the deal! If they take your book, you will usually need to do some publicity—newspaper, radio, or TV appearances—to boost sales.

> "A good book proposal is a narrative outline. When you do one, you've done the work of outlining the book, killed two birds with one stone."
>
> **—NICHOLAS BAKALAR**

4. Once you have a manuscript, go for the throat—write, call, visit, email, plead, beg, pray, and do all you can to get them to read it.

If you send a manuscript in or a publisher asks to see it, give it your best shot. The more appealing your manuscript is when they first see it, the better its chance of selling (and you rarely get a second chance at the same publisher). I like to include some artwork in my drafts, and even lay them out and spiral-bind them. Do whatever you can to make your book stand out from all those others that get mailed to them every day!

> "Even the best book will not sell itself—you have to go out and blow your own horn."
>
> **—ROHN ENGH, author, photographer, and photomarketer**

5. You can approach many publishers at the same time. Given how slow the whole process can be, it only makes sense to do so, and they expect it. It's helpful to note in your letter that it's a simultaneous submission.

6. Don't give up… it's that simple—if you don't give up, you won't fail.

The size of the town has nothing to do with the size of the people!

Wall Street is not Main Street!

The little rancher's cow tastes as good as the big rancher's beef.

It's not the size of the dog in the fight, it's the size of the fight in the dog.

I've assembled these "big vs. little" sayings to help convince you that no matter how small and insignificant your book may seem (in comparison to Dean Koontz's latest blockbuster), it does have some merit and some chance out there.

REJECTION

Many would-be writers never recover from their first rejection letter. But rejection for the most part is a no-brain process. A rejection slip is no different from discovering that the local restaurant is closed when your mouth was all set for one of its salad bars. You'll recover in a couple of minutes and probably find a better deal (or meal) elsewhere.

Just don't quit trying. I struggle with my fortieth book just as you may with your first. But I **will** sell it, somewhere, because I won't quit trying. If the message is important to me, it will be to others—someday! So if I get nowhere with a book or proposal after a determined series of submissions, I lay it aside until I find a fit or its time comes.

If you love your book and it is worthy enough, you will sell it someday. Many farmers make a profit, and marriages get better, someday.

"I've had three rather successful books, but each book has had one or two editors write back after receiving a proposal that 'this book would be of no help to any patient' (this was *Overcoming Depression,* now in its third edition and just nominated by the National Alliance for the Mentally Ill as one of the twelve most important books on mental health in the past decade); or 'No parent will ever buy this book,' and 'It will never sell more than 8,000 copies in hardcover' (this was in response to my proposal for *The Bipolar Child*). When the book was written, not only did parents buy it, but they bought six, eight, and ten copies at a time. '20/20' and Oprah featured it, and we sold 60,000 copies in hardcover within the first three months!"

—*JANICE PAPOLOS, author and self-taught publicist*

BOOK CONTRACTS

If your book is accepted by a publisher, you will receive a contract from it.

Book contracts are all much the same, and in general they are strongly slanted in the publisher's favor. The average book contract is not looking after your interests any more than it absolutely has to. The key things to pay attention to in a book contract are:

1. ROYALTIES—What will the publisher pay by way of royalties, and are they based on retail price or the publisher's selling cost (net receipts)? There is a big difference in dollars and cents between the two—retail is much better (see "net receipts" in the Glossary).

Some publishers, on the other hand, will pay only net royalties. If this is a publisher in a strong position to sell your book (your book is on guppy breeding, and it has a big line of pet specialty books sold in every pet store across the country), it may still be worth your while over time. If you must accept a net royalty, at least try for more smaller "steps" or escalations until you reach the highest rate in the sliding scale.

The royalties on hardcover editions are usually higher than those on paperbacks. (See page 106.)

Read all the fine print of the royalty clause carefully because there are often lower royalties on various special categories of sales, such as mail-order sales and high-discount and premium sales. You might ask the publisher what percent of its sales are likely to be in the regular edition and what by these special channels to get a better idea of the **actual** royalty rate.

Publishers usually pay royalties twice a year.

2. ADVANCE—As noted earlier, an advance is a lump sum of money paid by the publisher to the author. You might call it an upfront payment to seal the bargain and testify to the fact that both intend to fulfill their end of the bargain (the author will write the book, and the publisher publish it). An advance gets its name from the fact that this money is advanced from the royalties the book is expected to earn.

The amount of the advance depends on how converted the publisher is to you and your works. Advances go from $1,000 to a couple million (if you happen to be a celebrity), but most first book advances, especially for an unagented book, are somewhere between $3,000-$10,000. Advances are usually paid in installments, such as half when you sign the contract and when the finished manuscript has been accepted by the publisher. Publishers must recoup the advance through book sales before you see any further money from royalties.

I've made it clear that I don't like advances myself because it usually means you are getting paid ahead for something you haven't done—which means lots of pressure. In a very real sense it is a "debt" to the publisher, not paid until you successfully deliver an acceptable manuscript. Others count on advances for money to eat on while they write a book. Your call. Just remember, it's your money and after the first year's sales, you may get nothing more, as many books barely "earn out" their advance. Whether or not you want an advance, and how much, may depend on your tax situation (when would it be the most advantageous—or disadvantageous—to get the money?).

If you take a firm stand, you can usually lever a publisher up at least a little from its initial advance offer. In any case, the royalty rate is more important in the long run than what the advance happens to be.

2. SUBSIDIARY RIGHTS—These are the other things the publisher might like to do with your book besides publish it in the original edition—such as let it be published in other countries, used in book clubs and information retrieval systems, converted to audiotape, made into a movie, or used as the basis for new toy series.

The contract sent to a first-time author will usually give the publisher a wide range of such rights, with the proceeds of any such uses split 50/50 between publisher and author. Experienced authors and those who have made a name for themselves, and/or who have agents, will often withhold some of these rights or go for a higher percentage of the profits. Unless you have a very hot property, you may just want to leave things in the publisher's favor the first time around. If you want to inform yourself and argue about some of the subsidiary rights, see *Kirsch's Guide to the Book Contract,* by Jonathan Kirsch.

3. COPYRIGHT—The publisher will take care of filing the copyright for you, but it should of course be in your name.

4. NONCOMPETE CLAUSE—What right do you have to write anything on a similar or related topic once they publish your book? Generally, you have to be careful here and get the publisher's permission if necessary. This is a fair restriction to put on the author because the publisher doesn't want you out selling another book that's going to undercut the book you just sold it. But do check the wording of the "noncompete" clause and make sure it is not **too** restrictive.

5. INDEMNITY or "hold harmless" clause—The publisher doesn't want any trouble, and it doesn't want to be liable for any mistakes you might make that may cost them money. This one is hard to get changed in any way, but at least try to make sure that you are responsible for actual breaches only of this clause, not merely alleged breaches.

6. PERMISSIONS—If you are including any appreciable amount of copy from other published sources in your book, the publisher will insist on having written permission from the copyright holder on same by the time it has your finished manuscript. See "fair use" in the Glossary.

7. MANUSCRIPT—This clause will specify how long the finished manuscript is supposed to be (how many words), and how many and what kind of illustrations, if any, you are supposed to provide with it. It

will note the date you're supposed to deliver all this by, and how long after this you have before they can cancel the contract for nondelivery.

Publishers don't like to pay for illustrations, but if illustrations are important to your book, and expensive, see if you can persuade them to at least share the cost in some way (beg if you have to!).

Many contracts make it clear that whether the book is "acceptable" (covers the right subject in the right way) is a judgment that will be made entirely by them. At least try to make sure you have the right to revise the manuscript to their specifications if they find it unacceptable.

8. PUBLICATION—This clause will specify the time period within which the publisher will publish your book. Bear in mind that book publishers in general move slowly, but don't let them say more than eighteen months here unless you wouldn't mind posthumous publication.

9. AUTHOR'S REVIEW OF BOOK STAGES—Most publishers will allow you to review the copyedited manuscript (see chapter ten), and proofs and will give you a time limit for these operations. And if you monkey too much with the proofs (make changes that affect more than 10 percent of the type), it will cost you.

10. INDEX—Publishers usually want you to do the index, or to pay for someone they hire to do it. No harm in asking if they will assume this cost.

11. REVISION—Should your book be lucky enough to have a long life, the publisher will eventually want you to revise it. If a revision is going to require a lot of work, they should give you at least a modest advance for it.

12. AUTHOR'S DISCOUNT for copies purchased. Get as good a discount as you can on copies of your book you will be buying from them—at least 40 and maybe 50 percent. Most publishers will give a higher discount (up to perhaps 65 percent) if you buy in quantity.

13. OVERSTOCK OR REMAINDER COPIES—Be sure this clause gives you the right to buy any overstock or remainder copies at "the best price obtainable from any third party."

14. REVERSION OF RIGHTS—Most contracts will list various conditions under which you can ask for the rights to the book to be reverted to you, such as bankruptcy, failure to pay royalties, or the book

goes out of print. Be sure to get the right to buy all of the printing materials at manufacturing cost or less so you can produce your book yourself once it belongs to you again.

15. OPTION (right of first refusal)—The contract may give the publisher the option to your next book, or next book on a similar subject. You may feel comfortable with this, or even flattered by it, as long as it is expressed in a way that doesn't box you in too much, such as they have the right to publish your next book "on terms not less favorable than those offered by a thrid party."

The morning after!

With publishers, there is a tomorrow. Never forget that. There are plenty of publishers out there, but this industry is still a small world. Your publishers are your friends—they want your book to sell even more than you do (you have your heart in this, but they have their money and reputation on the line, too). The romance of getting the big "yes," from them, signing the contract, getting an advance, and getting your book out is often tested later when sales results come in and your authorial enthusiasm needs someone to blame or to beat on when things slow down... and they generally do.

When this happens, asking "what can we do about this" rather than "what are you going to do about it" is the best way to keep your "marriage" intact. When things go wrong or are disappointing, don't whine, criticize, second-guess, or threaten to change publishers. The more your publisher likes you, the more attention your book will get in the maze of the many others it has. Let me share with you some of the things I've done along this line:

1. Keep your publisher posted on what you are doing by way of publicity, when, and where, so it can coordinate its own efforts with yours, including shipping to, or calling nearby bookstores to be sure your book is available for your audience to buy.

2. When traveling, visit bookstores, make friends with the clerks, and autograph any copies of your book you find there. I've even quietly rearranged things so that my books were face out, or in front!

3. Sell as many books on your own as you can—it shows the publisher that you love your own book and are willing to push it.

4. Volunteer for media and speaking appearances.

5. Send your editor or publicist copies of any media attention your book gets—articles, tapes, etc. They often can find more important uses for these than just decorating your own wall or scrapbook.

6. Stop by and see them when you're in the area so they know you are alive.

7. Have the attitude that **you** carry the burden of the book. After all, it is your book—the publisher is helping you with it and investing in you.

8. After your first book is out, ask if there's a second one you could do, or ask about any additional book ideas you have yourself. I can thank my editors (especially good old Carol) for many of my additional book ideas.

8. Help your publisher promote other authors' books (yes, the other guy's book) whenever you can. It will please the publisher, not hurt the sale of your book, and may get you some reciprocal publicity in return.

In general, keep an open and positive relationship with your publisher, whether your first book with them is a big success or not, and it won't end up a "one-book stand."

CHAPTER 10

A Short Course in Self-Publishing

Self-publishing your own book is a big subject that I can't cover in complete detail here. There are several good guides to the subject, including *The Complete Guide to Self-Publishing*, by Tom and Marilyn Ross, and *The Self-Publishing Manual,* by Dan Poynter. Let me just tell you enough here so that you can decide which path to pursue.

Options for "Operation Book"

If you decide to do your own book, you can take any of these approaches.

1. Do it **entirely yourself**, by trial and error. Depending on how much you know about the process, this can be a little risky. But it will be a real education.

2. Get **some help from others**—some ideas and leads from what you read here, and the other sources I've suggested, and orchestrate the whole thing yourself, finding specialists to help you with specialized parts of the process as necessary (editors, designers, book printers, etc.).

3. Go to a **vanity press** to have your book done. What's a vanity press? These are companies that, for an agreed-upon amount of money (not likely to be small), will take your manuscript and then give you a

finished book. You may have seen ads for vanity presses in magazines. They may create the impression that they will actually publish your book, but they will really only be producing it. The drawback here is that sometimes what comes out the other end is not a thing of beauty, and vanity presses are no real help with actually selling your book. They do often offer some marketing and publicizing services as part of what they do, but these are usually token and there is such a stigma attached to vanity presses that, for example, no reviewer will review a book produced by them. You need to be sure, too, that an agreement with a vanity press specifies that all the books in your order will be bound, not just printed.

4. Get a **custom book producer** to help you. These folks will help you with all or part of the book publishing process, as you desire. They can help you plan and execute the entire undertaking—both producing the book and marketing it afterward, or just assist with one or more stages you're uncertain about. Most custom book producers offer services such as the following:

manuscript critiques	proofreading
writing or ghostwriting	registering for copyright,
content editing	getting CIP data, and other
line editing/copyediting	important technicalities
illustrating	printing your book
cover design	book marketing
book interior design	publicity

(Check the Glossary for any terms you are unsure about in the above list.)

You can probably hire a custom book producer to help you for no more than it would cost to have a vanity press produce your book, and you will retain full control of your book and like the result better. Some good custom book producers are listed in the Resource List at the back of this book.

5. Go to a **short-run book printer,** and have them help you. Short-run printers (listed in a number of the books included in the Resource List, including *Literary Market Place*) often offer shortcuts to reduce costs, such as standard book designs and cover designs you can pick from or customize to your book. They can also take care of technical details such as filing copyright and getting bar codes for you and may produce materials such as posters and brochures to help promote your

book, if you desire. They will not get involved much in editorial aspects, but they know all about the production side. The final book you end up with here may be less classy and unique than one customized from start to finish (such as by a custom book producer), but it will be cheaper—maybe much cheaper.

6. Work with an **on-demand printer**. These are companies that can quickly produce just the number of copies of a book you need—even if that's only fifty—and print more whenever you need them, in quantities small or large. Their "printing" is done by a high-quality copier, and the finished product is hard to distinguish from a book done by regular offset printing. With this method you don't have to worry about storing big quantities of books (or getting stuck with them). Though the cost per copy is high, you can have an overall smaller investment because you don't have to print 5,000 or even 1,000. On-demand printers work from same thing you would send to a regular printer—an electronic file containing the finished, typeset, laid-out book. On-demand books can contain illustrations but no interior color. You may also have to pay a "setup fee" (usually under $500) as well as pay for any copies of your book you buy.

Some on-demand printers will have you sign a very publisherlike contract in which they agree to make your book available to the public (including online) and to publicize it in various ways, as well as to produce it, and to pay you royalties on sales. Even if there are no charges, or extra charges, for these marketing efforts, don't necessarily expect this to be quite the same as publishing with a conventional book publisher. You will get your book in print quickly, and they may "get it out there" some, but you may also find your right to the book compromised should you ever decide to move to full-scale traditional publication.

7. There is also an option that you might call **self-publishing through a publisher.** These are some publishers around who will run your book through their system (edit it, produce it, put it in their catalogs, send it out for review, etc.) IF you pay them a healthy stipend to do so. You will probably get a decently edited and professional-looking product, but they may not be as much help as you imagined with actually getting it sold. This is also called co-op, or subsidy, publishing.

8. If you don't care whether you have a physical book in your hands

and just want to get your ideas and information out there, you may consider doing an **ebook**. The guides listed in the Resource List will help you here.

Remember, folks, in all of these choices you are working simply to get your first book out, so even if some of these options end up a little worse than you sought, that isn't the end of the world or of your book career. If your book idea and desire to do it are strong enough, minor failures or a few bad decisions are not going to destroy you. It all counts toward building your competence as a writer and helping you perhaps someday to set up your own little publishing company for other books you will do. That little pen in hand can beat any key or credit card in hand because it makes you a *creator*.

Packaging and presentation

When you start planning your self-publishing project, you need to think about what your book will look like, not just what it will say.

One of my cleaning company managers, Jim Warnock, did a little demonstration once that I'd like to share with you to make a point about the choices you have when it comes to presenting your book to readers.

Jim bought two chocolate cakes and set them in front of the audience, pointing out that they were exactly the same—size, ingredients, taste, and calories. He said "Now I'm going to serve Mr. Smith here in the front row a piece of this cake." Jim then walked over to the first cake and with his bare hand brutally tore a big handful out of one side of the cake and boldly walked over and slammed it into (well dressed) Mr. Smith's hand. It was so awful that a groan went up from the audience. "Now that's one way," said Jim, "I got the job done, didn't I? He got the cake." The audience agreed. Then he put on a white dinner jacket, put a napkin over his arm, put the other cake on a dazzling white platter, set the platter on a tray and walked over to the person sitting next to Smith. He set down the tray, spread out the snowy napkin, carefully set the platter in the center, laid some silverware out nicely, and lit a candle. Then with a shining spatula he cut a generous piece out of the cake, carefully placed it on a handsome plate, bowed, and gave it to the gentleman. In both cases, as he pointed out to the audience, he did exactly the same thing—got the cake to the customer—but HOW he did it was the difference.

Think about this now. How are you going to serve up your thoughts and information to the audience? Will it be just the facts, or made classy and appetizing with attractive design and layout?

A pretty book—take a look

We are living in day of visuals like we never imagined—a simple thirty-second commercial has two dozen or more well-done scenes, costing up to millions to make. The combination of sound, sight, color, and special effects is so amazing that even the most blasé of us shake our heads in awe. So how is a little book printed on paper with dull black ink going to compete with all this? It isn't! People are used to pizazz. People are lazy lookers and readers now. Information comes too easy, and we are assaulted with thousands of glamorized bits of it every day, from all sides. Where does your little book with its big message fit into this overoffered, overstimulated, overloaded society? It doesn't. You have to make it fit, using every trick and bit of wit and creativity you have so that people will notice, buy, read, and like your book, and then tell their friends about it.

The people—from Disney to Discovery Channel—who do manage to reach into the minds and hearts of us all do it by DESIGN, packaging things to be picked up, making them seductive enough to make us reach for our wallets. Straight type won't do it any more.

Design is a big part of marketing just about everything—cars, clothes, tools, and appliances. The actual function of things is almost secondary to what they look like. Even warranties and instruction sheets are often attractively designed.

Your book has to compete with this kind of appeal, so it has to be attractive outside and when you open it up, too. As you go along writing, collecting, and building your book, you also need to think about what could help make this book LOOK GOOD.

With the graphic capacities of our computers and other machines today and their amazing programs, it's not hard make our pages pretty as well as palatable.

I think of a page as a painting, a landscape of information to look at before you read it. That makes you **want** to read it! I could go on about this forever, but instead let me SHOW you the difference. Look at the different presentations of exactly the same material below. It doesn't take a rocket scientist to figure out which will catch the eye and be read. These pages contain exactly the same words, but look at the difference in them.

Get the picture?

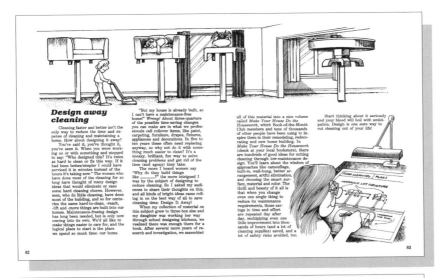

Design away cleaning

Cleaning faster and better isn't the only way to reduce the time and expense of cleaning and maintaining a home. How about designing it away?

You've said it, you've thought it, you've seen it. When you were working on or with something and stopped to say: "Who designed this? It's twice as hard to clean or fix this way. If it had been better/simpler I could have serviced it in minutes instead of the hours it's taking now." The women who have done most of the cleaning for so long have thought of many design ideas that would eliminate or ease some hard cleaning chores. However, men, who do little cleaning, have done most of the building, and so for centuries the same hard-to-clean, -reach, -lift and -move things are built into our homes.

Maintenance-freeing design has long been needed, but is only now coming into its own. We'd all like to make things easier to care for, and the logical place to start is the place we spend so much time: our home.

"But my house is already built, so I can't have a maintenance-free home!" Wrong! About three-quarters of the possible time-saving changes you can make are in what we professionals call rollover items, like paint, carpeting, furniture, drapes, fixtures, appliances and decorations. In five to ten years these often need replacing anyway, so why not do it with something easier to clean? It's a sneaky, brilliant, fun way to solve cleaning problems and get rid of the time (and agony) they take.

The more I heard women say "Why do they build things like _____?", the more intrigued I was by the subject of designing to reduce cleaning. So I asked my audiences to share their thoughts on this, and all kinds of bright ideas came rolling in on the best way of all to save cleaning time: Design It Away!

When my collection of material on this subject grew to three-box size and my daughter was working her way through school designing kitchens, we realized there was enough there for a book. After several more years of research and investigation, we assembled all of this material into a nice volume called *Make Your House Do the Housework*, which Book of the Month Club members and tens of thousands of other pepole have been using to inspire them in their remodeling, redecorating, and new home building. In *Make Your House Do the Housework* (check at your local bookstore), there are hundreds of good ideas for cutting cleaning through low-maintenance design. You'll learn about the wisdom of approaches like camouflage, built-in, wall-hung, better arrangement, artful elimination, and choosing the smart surface, material, and color. The thrill and beauty of it all is that when you change even one single thing to reduce its maintenance requirements, those savings in time and effort are repeated day after day, multiplying even one little improvement into thousands of hours (and a lot of cleaning supplies) saved, and a lot of safety risks avoided.

Start thinking about it seriously and your blood will boil with anticipation. Design is one sure way to cut cleaning out of your life!

A spread from No Time to Clean!, *enlivening the subject of "Spot Cleaning."*

This, folks, is called book layout and design, and we do a lot of it ourselves right here in the office. But we have outside professionals do some of it, too, and it's money well spent. If an outsider is designing for us, we send him a copy of the manuscript, and a description of what we want the book to be like. Then he reads the manuscript and gives some book design ideas and samples of art styles he thinks might work for this book and we pick the ones we like best.

> *Book design is a process many people aren't aware of, but it makes a big difference in a book.*

Things to consider in a book design

- What the target audience is, and their age and sex.
- What the "trim size" of the book (see page 136) will be.
- The basic typeface (or "text" style), which most of the words in your book will appear in. Text type should not be smaller than ten point or bigger than eleven point. Do you want the pages to have one or two columns of type?

128

• How big (how many pages) you want the final book to be—do you need to stretch the copy out or pack it in?

• The kind of feeling or personality you want your book to have, flashy or dignified, for instance.

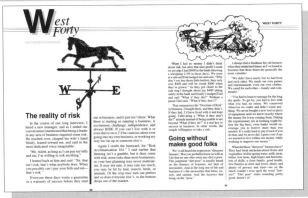

The chapter opening pages of three different books, with three different personalities.

• The headings (to break things up and help the reader find what he's looking for).

• The kind of illustrations the book will have, and how many.

I love graphics, charts, and art in a book. Notice how different all of the following layouts/pages from my books are.

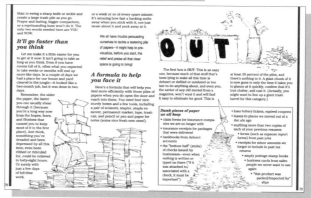

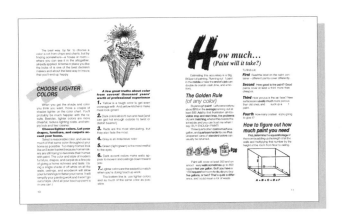

I love walking through bookstores and just looking at the thousands of different designs and layouts. When you find one that really catches your eye and turns you on, use it as a starting point for your own thoughts on design.

Getting your book designed

Book design is important, but don't get shook by this part of bookdom you may have never considered before. There are no big secrets or unbreakable rules here and not much expense. Design is just a little thing that makes a big difference in a book.

I've seen superbly designed and illustrated books that said little or nothing—they were just tinsel and flash—had no significant message or content. And I've seen poorly designed books, actually ugly, that we can't put down. So just be aware of the fact that design can be a big boost to a strong message.

A freelance designer can help you here, or you can use one of the computer design programs such as PageMaker or Quark Xpress. A typesetter at your local print shop will do a good job if you provide samples of the look you want. You don't have to reinvent the wheel here, come up with something that's never been done before. Just look at a variety of books, and choose the elements you like from each.

Book designers choose "book" fonts for the body of your book. These are long-used, time-honored type styles that can be read page after page, chapter after chapter without strain. If you choose something funky that gives readers a headache after about a page and a half, you've defeated your purpose.

If you decide to use a designer, you can find one by calling the art department of a publisher, small press, university press, or even a regional magazine near you, and asking for a recommendation. Freelance book designers are also listed in *Literary Market Place* under "Artists & Art Services."

If they agree to take on the job, be sure to show them any formats, layouts, and type treatments you've seen in other books and liked. It's also helpful to go through the manuscript before sending it off to them and make a list of all the major "design elements." This means the things you would like to have a distinct style of their own—anything you would like to stand out from the text proper. A designer may not create a separate style for everything you list (one of her jobs is to make a book look handsome and consistent, not TOO chopped up with different styles), but it will alert her to everything she might consider.

Here is a sample list of this type:

MARSH CREEK PRESS
A division of Don Aslett Inc.

Dear Designer:

The following is a list of the design elements in the manuscript at present.

HEADLINES:
I've used three levels of headline, so we will need an A Head, B head, and C head.

LIST FORMATS:
plain lists
bulleted lists
numbered lists

BOXES:
Regular Boxes
Big boxes or sidebars

QUOTES FROM OTHERS
These appear throughout the book, and it would be nice to have these distinguished clearly from the text proper: with a different type style, screening, whatever.

SIMULATED "LETTER" FORMAT:
For the letters I am reproducing in the manuscript, see pages 32, 117, and 297.

SPECIAL TYPE WITHIN TEXT
I would like an occasional bit of copy (phrase or sentence) to stand out in the text, such as on pages 16, 44, and 89.

I'll look forward to hearing from you after you've had a chance to look this all over.

Sincerely,

Don Aslett

PO BOX 700
POCATELLO
IDAHO 83204

311 S FIFTH AVE
POCATELLO
IDAHO 83201

PH 208-232-3535
FX 208-235-5481

*Some examples
of conventional
book design.*

CHAPTER 4

The Big Step: Getting Started

YOU'VE GOT TO START SOMEWHERE . . .

The world is full of people who want and wish to write, but never start. Starting seems to be the biggest obstacle in writing. Too many would-be writers scare themselves silly mulling it over and over, worrying and wondering, listening to horror stories and talking to others about all the negatives. Or believing exaggerated success stories that make writing sound impossible for them.

It's like building that dream house. People want it, and build it in their mind, talk about it, promise themselves and others that it will be done. But years slip by waiting for the perfect time and the perfect property, the perfect plan. In any area of our lives or aspirations, things don't just come together by themselves.

But once you put the money down on a piece of property and then walk around out on it on Sunday afternoon and pace it out and put a stake down where the house will go, magic happens. Everything begins to move and flow.

Great books or articles don't just come, either. Nothing just happens in writing—you have to make it happen. Waiting for everything you've been dreaming of to come showering down on you from an idea and handful of notes is futile thinking.

You can't wait to work everything out before getting to work. Never wait to start something important, something you really want to do. Starting has its own power—it welds you to the event, the desire. Starting is the official proof to yourself and others that you are really going to do it, which in turn makes all kinds of resources appear. Thinking it over, and even fantasy and daydreams (which you ought to

take notes on), are good for a writer. But when the time comes to write, then write. You accomplish more through movement than meditation. Timidness in writing gets tiresome, not just to you, but to all those people you've been telling about your "someday" book for decades now.

At some point, you've got to quit sampling and circling and just bite off a chunk and chew. You learn to fight—and organize—in battle much faster and better than you do forever thinking it over.

Being afraid of writing is downright ridiculous. Who and what is going to hurt you? And writing is a low-capital investment. If you do it and lose it, or have to rip it up and start again, or it doesn't sell, or no one likes it, you aren't out much but ego (which may not be all bad). You did get some experience and a chance to set up some good habits and systems. Maybe this first fling was just the audition for the great book or article coming in the next team of pages. No writing is wasted. A painter's best painting owes a debt to the thirty-eight terrible ones that came before.

You just cannot have the best, the most, or for that matter anything without *starting*. Right now, at two A.M. if necessary, during the worst part of your pregnancy, right after you've been fired, during your divorce, while struggling with your diet, when you are sixteen, when you are sixty-eight, or while it is raining.

WAITING ONLY MAKES IT HARDER

Many people say to me, when I ask them about the little writing assignment I gave them for a brochure, newsletter, catalog or the like, "I haven't got to it yet, but it's sitting right here on my desk." Sitting isn't ready. Sitting isn't going anywhere. And worse, **the longer something sits, the older it gets, and the harder it is to do.** Staleness turns off a writer, or anyone else. It's true that finding the time, the tools, the place and the mood is all part of getting ready and organized to write, but starting will get you on your way and marshal these more effectively than anything!

Once you begin to write, it's amazing how much will just come. I'm a big believer in roughing things—just getting what you have to say down in any form at first. As you're doing this, new angles, new approaches, new aspects of the subject and entirely new ideas will flash into your mind. Don't let these distract or derail you, just jot them down on a separate pad and stick with your original focus. Once you have that down, go back and flesh out your new idea. Just watch—while

---

I f you E-mail similar material frequently, use your word-processing software to create your own "Personalized Speed Macro" form.

❖ ❖ ❖ ❖

I f it's not possible to get a letter typed or printed, a handwritten note may be not only effective, but even more personal and graceful.

❖ ❖ ❖ ❖

E ven with the aid of the swift and tireless computer, correcting things takes time. How many errors justify revising and reprinting a letter you thought was ready to go? One hand-done correction on a piece of correspondence is okay — in fact it adds a personal touch, as well as the assurance that you actually read it before it went out.

❖ ❖ ❖ ❖

D on't apologize at length in a business letter for something minor, such as delay in answering. It wastes time, and just reminds readers of their irritation. They've heard from you at last, and what they're really interested in is the point, which you have not yet gotten to! If you feel apologizing is essential, do it just once, briefly — and remember that one *good* excuse is usually better than two or three.

❖ ❖ ❖ ❖

W hen registering complaints, brevity beats the blow-by-blow. "We relied on you and it didn't turn

out well" is usually better than taking the time and energy to get down all the details, eager as you may be to immortalize every irritating shortcoming.

❖ ❖ ❖ ❖

T hanks to those marvelous computers, we can send formal letters or E-mail to forty-two people in no time flat, just by popping in names and addresses. This operation is so simple it's almost brainless, wherein lies the catch: It's all too easy to ship out the wrong message or materials packet to the wrong person. Always double-check before you post or transmit!

ACRONYMS AND JARGON

When I see an ASAP
What does that symbol mean to me?
Some codes, such as these FYIs,
Seem understood by other guys.
As for FOB, I might decipher this
But AOL-LOL I surely miss.
"ADC pulled a JIT" — what are you really
   telling me?
"ID the V/SOT" is total Greek, you see.
Acronyms and jargon are new and nineties
   — hot!
But more efficient? ITN! (I think not!)

78 ❖ Keeping Work Simple

Corresponding ❖ 79

---

*Most books have "headlines,"
but you can use your
imagination here, too.*

S PRAY PAINTING

It looks so fast, so easy, on TV and watching the pros do it. But 95% of the time when ordinary people try it, the National Guard has to be called in before they're through. (I painted 300 cars once, inadvertently, while doing one roof!)

Spray painting is fast and easy IF:
• You have lots of easily accessible footage to paint.
• You have a high quality gun and any necessary scaffolding.

You can rent a nice airless unit, fairly trouble free, for about $40 a day. You'll have less overspray with an airless sprayer, because you aren't spraying a mixture of paint and air, but 100% pure paint.

**Your "watch outs"
here are:**

1. Keeping fallout—drift and overspray—to a minimum. In the kind of painting it's ESPECIALLY important to cover up anything you don't want painted. Be extra careful outdoors, where with the slightest breeze

paint can easily drift onto other people's property. Don't spray on windy days, or around corners.

2. Keeping the paint perfectly clean—even a mosquito eyebrow in there will plug the nozzle. Paint stores have filters that will help out here. With spray paint you need to be especially sure to follow the manufacturer's mixing and thinning directions.

3. Make sure the area is well ventilated. And wear a respirator and/or safety glasses if you need to.

4. Remember that pressure! Airless spray guns are wonderful and they work well without air because the paint or whatever is in there is under 1500-3000 pounds of pressure from a highly efficient pump. This shoots out a stream of paint like a needle, so never point the gun at anyone, including yourself (don't look at it while it's running to see if the nozzle is clear, for instance). Never leave the gun sitting anywhere while the machine is on. Guns of any kind are always an attraction for kids and they will pick them up to play with them. A spray machine like this can maintain a dangerous amount of pressure even when it's off, so always release or bleed off the pressure before leaving the gun anywhere.

Wear a stocking cap and rub a little Vaseline on your face before you start. It protects you and makes cleaning the paint up and off a LOT easier.

41

134

A few years ago I decided to publish a book largely composed of the many astounding letters and comments I'd received from readers about clutter—*Clutter Free! Finally & Forever*. After considering the options, we decided to use a mix of typefaces (to highlight the many different voices here). This can be a little iffy if not done carefully, but it came out pleasantly readable in this case.

I like to include some "shocker" pages in my books to really get the reader's attention or hammer home a point I think is important. Your book should be readable and attractive, but it doesn't have to be exactly like everyone else's.

Charts, illustrated step-by-step sequences, and other graphics liven up a book, raise reader interest, and help bring your message home. My own books are well known for their charts, quizzes, and checklists.

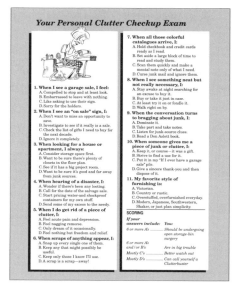

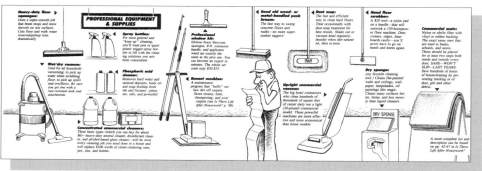

Trim size (is there a wise size?)

Here again you have options. The size (in books this is called the "trim size") you pick for your book is really a place for common sense, not romanticism. The family history book my mother did, for example, needed to display photographs well and to be set on a coffee table and read easily even by those who need larger print. So we picked a nice big 8.5 x 11. Some little "quick-read" or carry along books work well in a 4 x 6 or even smaller format. Plain text or "reading" books are often 6 x 9.

A book's size will often depend on the number and type of illustrations in it, and whether there are things like forms, graphs, and charts that need to be effectively presented.

Bear in mind that straying from printers' standard sizes will cost you because of extra charges to adjust the press setup and less efficient use of paper. Standard book sizes include 5.25 inches x 8, 6 x 9, 8 x 10, and 8.5 x 11, for instance.

Try not to use unusual sizes unless they're really necessary—check with the printer you have in mind first to see what sizes are most economical. With a copy of your manuscript in hand, visit a book printer, and in a few minutes they can quote you the costs of using the size you have in mind, vs. a wiser size if there is one.

If you feel strongly about a certain size, however, go for it because your book is going to be around a long time and you want to be happy with it. I've adopted a size for many of my books—7 x 9—that my printer calls Aslett format (nice to have a size named after you!). It allows room for all the illustrations my books usually have, sticks out a little on the shelf (beyond the competition), and just feels and looks good to me.

A complaint I sometimes have against publishers is that they put too many pages in too small a trim size, making the book look thick and bulky. If they just chose a larger overall size, the book would be sleek and nice. So remember, your judgment could be as good as or better than theirs. No one owns book size.

A word about paper

When I self-published my first book and the staff at the printer asked me "What kind of stock do you want?" I thought they were talking about what I might do with my eventual book earnings. But no, it was the quality and type of paper. They showed me samples from newsprint to rag bond and beyond, and finally I chose the most expensive "coated" stock, which added 20 cents to the price of each book. Little did I know that most publishers are ultra-conservative here and often go for the cheapest and thinnest paper they can get by with without the type showing through.

The type of paper you choose will have a lot to do with whether your book has illustrations, and what kind.

Do remember when choosing paper that you don't want your book to look intimidating. My favorite of all my books, *Clutter's Last Stand*, came off the press at 288 pages, and it looked bulkier than the Old and New Testaments with commentary. People would look at it and say, "I want to be dejunked, but not that bad." The printer had used a thick paper (which on a skimpy book would be great). On the next printing it went to a thinner paper, and those 288 pages were reduced from three-quarters of an inch to five-eighths, and the book looked good and took off.

Consider the color of the paper, too. Have you ever used makeup that didn't match your complexion or clothes? Well, on my next decluttering book, done with the world's largest publisher, the off-white, almost gray paper color the publisher picked for the pages was off-putting to even my most faithful fans—it looked "dirty" to them. That was changed in the next printing, and it made a difference. However if you are doing a book called "The Backhoe Operators of America," a dirtlike tint may be just what you want! Just remember that when it comes to books, *readability* is the name of the game.

Binding

Depending on how big your book is (how many pages), you have options here.

A saddle-stitched binding or staples work best for books of less than sixty pages. A binding like this, however, has no real "spine" to put the title and author on, so the book may never be seen on a bookstore shelf. We like to imagine our book being displayed face out, but most books in today's crowded bookstores end up on the shelf spine out.

If shelf visibility is important, then even for a small book go to a "perfect binding," which means the book has a square spine that can be printed on, and the whole thing will look more booklike. And a perfect-bound book isn't much more expensive than a stapled and folded book.

Some books, such as cookbooks and other types of instruction books, need to lay flat and open, and books can be bound in such a way as to take this into account. Spiral bindings also work well for this purpose. There are both plastic and metal spiral bindings, but again, on many of these you can't print a title on the spine, so you are at a disadvantage on the shelf. And spiral bindings can be crushed in shipping. Ask your printer what lay-flat bindings they have available, such as Repkover, OTA, or Smyth sewn lay-flat bindings.

If you're doing a book to be used while cooking or doing household repairs, it may well have a different format than a book designed just for reading.

One thing you'll notice when looking at the thousands of different paperbacks around is how many different thicknesses and textures of cover stock there are. It's exciting to shop around and ask printers about the paper (or cardboard) choices here. You can get coated stock, shiny foil embossing and many others. For example if you are doing an investment or money book, there is a "certificate"-looking paper stock that says "money" to anyone picking it up. If you are doing a sewing book, there are cover materials that look like fabric. This is all a part of creating a good book, so do whatever you have to do make it look the best you can, the way you'd like to look when heading out for the big date or to close that big deal!

The illustration below shows books with case or cloth binding, perfect binding, and saddle-stitching.

Paperback or hardcover?

Books likely to be read once, such as the average novel, are generally paperback because paperbacks are considerably cheaper to print, you can get more of them into a shipping box, and they are less expensive to ship or mail. If you are doing a book that will be kept and used many times, however, then hardcover is surely an option. Hardback is more durable, and it seems expensive, lasting, and serious. If you think hardback would fit or sell your book better, consider it. Most of my books have been paperback because people think of cleaning as mundane and down to earth—it doesn't seem to have a hardcover spirit and price tag. Book clubs like hardcover books—they have often reprinted my paperbacks in hardcover for their own use.

Most hardcover books have a paper jacket as well, which includes sales copy about the book and the author. I'm not crazy about these as they are damaged easily and soon disappear, but on some kinds of books, they do seem to serve a purpose. If you don't want a jacket, you can consider a "self-cover" hardcover, also called paper over board, which has the jacket incorporated right into the cover and protected by a glossy coat of clear plastic.

PRICE

If you're self-publishing, deciding the retail price of your book is your call. I think many books are overpriced—$15–$30 just for something to read, and the textbook salespeople should have masks over their faces when they sell books to college and university students. I guess you get what the market will bear.

As for me, I like to hold that cover price down. Book wholesalers, book clubs, TV shopping channels, and other outlets who want a fat discount don't like this, but you can't please everyone! You need to price your book for its most likely audience—what will the readers you have in mind pay? Businesspeople in general are willing to pay more for books (because they can deduct them from their taxes, and they are willing to shell out for the golden secrets of getting ahead in business). For books in the home and household area, or in any subject that has a lot of competition, the prices are lower. The big onetime-event books by famous people who have done something very bad or good can get

$24.95 for the first month or year or so in print, and then they may be on the bargain book tables.

Take a good look around a few bookstores, and you'll get the picture. Impulse books (such as *Fifty Good Uses for a Dead Possum*) need to be under $10—the cheaper the better. The so-so, might-like books are $5–$15. The "think I really need this" books are $15–$25. The "I'm going to be a pro" or "to impress people" books are $30 and up. And some specialized and highly technical, or limited edition books can be $50–$100.

Most publishers multiply the manufacturing cost by a markup factor of somewhere between six and ten to get the selling price of a book. The manufacturing costs usually include typesetting, printing, binding, plates and other printing preparations. More expensive books can use a lower multiplier because the total number of dollars involved is greater.

As a self-publisher, which many of you may end up being, I like the $12–$15 price range. This means that if I print 5,000–10,000 copies, the manufacturing cost is about $1.30 a book. This gives me lots of room to discount, especially at my speaking engagements and seminars.

The number of books you print really influences their cost. For example in the case of my little *Clean in a Minute* book, the average price for 5,000+ copies is just under a dollar. For a "short run" of these (2,700 copies), I've paid as much as $1.72 a copy. And on a printing of 30,000 copies for a special sale to the Navy, I got the same book for 54 cents each. A BIG difference! For small quantities of a book, the cost will be $2.50 a copy and up. My own philosophy is to always over-print. Go for it! This forces me to worry a little and sell harder, and so far I've only ended up stuck with a few pallets.

On-demand printing (see pages 124 and 156) is one possible way out of the "how many can I print" crunch.

Since you know your subject (or should), then you should also know your audience, and this will guide you on the psychology of price. Bookstores like a 40 to 45 percent discount off the cover price, whole-salers want 50 to 60 percent off and Amazon.com wants a 55 percent discount, so price accordingly. I discount my books for back-of-the-room sales at my speaking engagements. In our catalog (which you can get by writing to Marsh Creek Press, Box 700, Pocatello ID 83204), we sell our books at retail price, but on purchases of more than a dozen copies, we start discounting a little, and for quantity purchases in the hundreds of copies, we go up to 50 percent. For a premium sale, such as 10,000 copies, we may give 65 or 70 percent. It's your book, your money, and your call.

ART and artists

As noted earlier, I love art in a book. In fact, I demand it. I believe it is the best money you can spend once your creative pen and tiring mind have done all they can for your subject and message.

Art has a thousand options, but it can be a waste if done poorly. So first you'll have to fight off all the "wish I was" artist relatives and friends (all those amateurs) and stick to artists of truly professional quality. I had my day of coloring book- and high school yearbook-quality art, and back in the 1960s and even the 1980s I got away with a little of this in my books and booklets. But today people are used to the best, and they expect it.

Art from my first publications— this is not the kind of art you want!

Once you've chosen a good artist, bear in mind that you don't just toss art into a book or shoehorn it in. You let it do what words can't do, and combine it with the text so it works for you as in the samples below.

This gives a book some class, makes it more interesting, and helps the reader get the message.

Layout

Even good art and a good book design will not necessarily produce an impressive finished product if the pages are not laid out carefully, one by one, to look their best. This is easy to do once you have a design. You use the design as a guide and then "jiggle" things around as necessary on each page and spread until they look good to the eye. This does take a bit of artistic instinct, which is why publishers often have the designer of the book do the layout as well. You can do an excellent job yourself if you have a flair for this sort of thing, and learn how to use one of the design and layout programs, such as PageMaker or Quark Xpress.

THE CURTAIN RAISERS AND DROPPERS of a book

(which book people call "front matter" and "back matter")

THE UPFRONT PAGES

Some parts of the "front matter" are strictly necessary, but many are optional. A lot of this is your call, but get readers into the book quickly and in a good mood. Don't get carried away with your philosophies or any of the details of your subject yet—let the book itself do that. Too concentrated a taste of anything is not what you want here. Remember that what they see and sample in the front matter can hook, or turn off, potential readers.

Title page

The title page is the official first page of a book, always on a right-hand page. It contains the title of the book, the subtitle and/or blurb if there is one, the name of the author and illustrator, and sometimes (such as in the case of a book with many contributors) the editor. The bottom of the page shows the publisher's name and/or logo, and often its address.

Title pages don't have to be boring, as these samples show.

Autograph page or "half-title"

An optional page that comes before the title page and includes the title, if not the subtitle. I call this the "autograph page" and won't do a book without one. Autographs sell books—people keep an auto-graphed book longer and show it around more.

I make sure the half-title has a small illustration on it and plenty of space for an inscription. I like to have some nice white space on the left-hand side of the top of the page. I'm right-handed, and this way I can rest my hand on the bottom of the page and sign it gracefully whether I'm standing or sitting. I recommend you do something like this at the beginning of your book.

Here are a couple of examples of autograph pages.

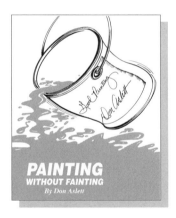

Copyright page

Here you put the copyright notice and the usual little statement about all rights reserved, no parts of this can be copied without permission, etc., and the Library of Congress Cataloging-in-Publica-tion data (see page 152). Here also go any notices required by people you had to get permissions from.

Dedication page

This page will bring out the romantic in most of us. Being able to dedicate all of your hard work on a book to someone is almost another whole reason to do one! Just bear in mind when composing dedications that your relationship with the parties in question might change or the sentiment become obsolete, yet there it still will be on 300,000 of your books.

If the dedication is not too long, it can be put on the copyright page, though the effect is not nearly as nice.

Acknowledgments

This is where you recognize anyone you want to recognize for their part in this undertaking—such as the editor, artist, designer, or agent and experts and helpers of all kinds.

Horn-tooting page

This is the "other books by this same author" page, where you list any other books you have done or anything that might enhance your credibility. Sometimes editors also put the "About the Author" in the front of the book (see page 148).

Introduction

Most books have an introduction. This is usually a strong, short summary of the need for the book, plus anything that underlines your credibility on the subject. You might even compliment the reader for buying the book and being interested in the subject. Best of all, when possible, is to make a BIG PROMISE as to what the book will do for them.

Below is the highly illustrated introduction to my classic book on decluttering, *Clutter's Last Stand*, and at the top of page 147, the introduction to *No Time to Clean!*

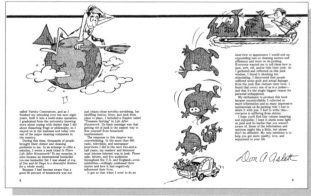

Foreword

I don't care for the common practice of having some other (preferably famous) person say good things about my book, when he or she probably hasn't even read it. If you do want one of these, make sure it's someone who can really do your book some good, and try to line up the person well ahead of time.

Table of contents

I like to have this on one page or a single spread whenever possible. Always design them so that they are attractive and easy to follow. A short salesy description of each chapter under the chapter title can help turn browsers into buyers.

The tables of contents for *Clutter's Last Stand* and *Painting Without Fainting*.

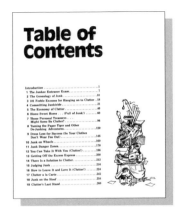

Table of Contents

TABLE OF CONTENTS

Epilogue

Many books have an epilogue, a minichapter or short piece at the end that sums up the book, recaps it, makes a revelation, or tells what happened later. This is the epilogue of *Who Says It's a Woman's Job to Clean?*, one of my favorites.

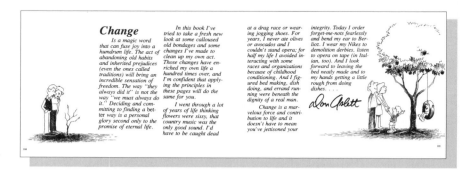

About the author

You need something short but strong here on your credibility in this subject, plus a photo if possible. I'd keep this to one page, for sure (you don't need to include your shoe size and all of your pets' names). This page may also appear near the front of the book.

Appendix or appendices

What usually goes into an appendix? Material that is related to your subject—good reference, background, or reinforcement of it—but too dull, technical, or detailed to put in the text proper.

Bibliography/book list

For more scholarly books this is a listing of all the sources you consulted when writing the book. Or it can be a list of books you recommend to the readers to expand their knowledge of your subject.

Index

An index is needed in any book that will be used for reference. If you don't want to do the index, let someone else who is thorough and methodical do it for you—someone else can often be more objective as to what-all is in there. There are many freelance indexers, listed in *Literary Market Place* and elsewhere, and at this writing they usually charge $3–$4 per book page to index. An index thoughtfully done by a human being is usually more useful than one done by computer.

Even an index can show some imagination.

Reader solicitation page

Most of my books also include a page in the back designed to solicit feedback from readers (and new real-life material for future books). Below are the reader solicitation pages from *Clutter Free! Finally and Forever; Get Organized, Get Published!;* and *The Office Clutter Cure.*

No need to dodge the legal bullets

All of those "credits" and copyrights and the like you see rolling on the screen before and after a movie are needed for a book, too. They are not a nuisance, they are there for the good of your book and you, and you can probably take care of them all in a couple of hours. So don't wrinkle your brow or go hire a lawyer. Just do it. Here are the basic things to be aware of here.

• **Copyright** Your book and everything in it is automatically protected by common law, but of course you want and need to register your copyright (preferably before you start distributing your book all over) to help prevent problems. For the details of how to do this call the U.S. Copyright Office, 202-707-3000, and ask for copyright package 109.

As it will tell you there, the copyright notice and symbol, and the name of the copyright holder, need to appear on your book's copyright page.

• **Disclaimer** If your book contains instructions or recipes, it's a good idea to have one of these in the front matter to reduce the chances of being sued when the crock pot explodes or your new mousetrap design catches someone's finger. You can check out the wording of the disclaimers used in books similar to yours, and it will give you the idea. The following is the covering-all-the-bases disclaimer from Dan Poynter's *Writing Nonfiction: Turning Thoughts into Books.*

• **Permissions** If you've quoted more than about 250 words verbatim from any book-length work, or 100 words from a published article, essay, or short story, you need to write to the publisher and ask permission to use it. This rule of thumb applies to regular text, not song lyrics or poems, which you have to be more careful about.

Send your request to the permissions department of the publisher. They move slowly but will usually grant it, sometimes for a fee, and give you the "permission granted" wording they want you to use in your book, often on the copyright page.

Don't get carried away with quotes from others, and permissions won't be a big problem. You don't want to let other people "carry" your book, anyway. Don't use quotes from others unless they're really needed and they absolutely fit.

• **Information important to libraries** There are two things here important to your book if you expect or want it to be sold in libraries.

First is the Library of Congress Cataloging Number, which goes on the copyright page of a new book and identifies it forevermore for libraries and their cataloging systems and review media. You can find out how to get this from the Cataloging in Publication Division of the Library of Congress at 202-707-6372, or http://pcn.loc.gov/pcn.

From the Library of Congress, you will also want to get CIP data for the copyright page. This is information (though it may look like Greek to us) that enables librarians to catalog our book quickly and easily. The snag here is that the Library of Congress won't give you CIP data until you've published three books. Until then you can get Quality Books (800-323-4241, or www.quality-books.com) to provide copy (called PCIP) that serves the same purpose, for a small fee.

• **ISBN** This is a number printed on the copyright page of your book and the back cover that unmistakably identifies your book amidst the millions of other books out there. Each edition of your book (paperback, hardcover, revised, etc.) will have its own ISBN. ISBNs are issued by R.R. Bowker, one of the great mother lodes of book publishing services and information. They can be reached at 800-521-8110 or www.isbn.org.

• **Bar code** This is a UPC (Universal Product Code) put on the backs of books to assist with inventory control in a bookstore, or anywhere. For a small fee, your designer or printer can get this for you. One inexpensive source of bar codes is Greenleaf Enterprises, Inc. (800-932-5420; www.greenleafenterprises.com).

THE BODY OF YOUR BOOK, OR "TEXT"

Copyediting

Copyeditors correct spelling and grammar and make sure you have commas, question marks, and colons in all the right places. They call any errors or oversights to your attention, smooth out your sentences where necessary, and check for small inconsistencies of many kinds. If you are being published by a publisher, a different editor from your main or "content" editor will often do the copyediting. If you are self-publishing, you need to find someone unfamiliar with the book to do it. Trying to copyedit yourself is hard because you are used to reading the meaning and not the words. Computers and all of their self-check programs do reduce the number of obvious errors in a manuscript, but they don't eliminate the need for copyediting.

You can ask a local newspaper, magazine, or book publisher to recommend some copyeditors. Copyeditors can also be found in *Literary Market Place* under "Editorial Services."

Proofreading

Here, too, being very familiar with the book can be a real handicap. You're so used to reading it you can and will read right over an error again and again, while it jumps right off the page for an outsider. Computers can't find all the errors either, no matter how many spellchecking or Mac-whatever programs they have. I've seen books edited and proofed four times, and a good proofreader can go behind them and find all kinds of other little mistakes. If there are too many errors in the finished book, this may undermine its credibility.

Proofreaders cost $12–$15 or sometimes more an hour, but it is worth it! By the way, when the preefer tells you how much he loved the book, take this with a grane of salt—well-done proofing gives you little chance to read in the orddinary sense!

By the way, did you catch the error(s) in that last paragraph? You did? Great—but you still need a proofreader.

Going to press

Now it's almost time to print your book, and those big questions come forth:
- Where?
- How much?
- How many?

What you want for your book is a full-service book manufacturer, which means a printer that specializes in book production and printing. While book publishing professionals sometimes have good reasons for buying paper, printing, binding, and other services from different suppliers, and then scheduling and coordinating all of these details themselves, most books are made by printers who specialize in producing books and take care of all of these other aspects in the process.

As a self-publisher, this is the kind of printer you want. Better yet is to find a book manufacturer that specializes in the kind of book you want to publish (short run, paperback, full color, whatever). This is the best way to ensure an attractive, reasonably priced, professional-looking product. The book manufacturer will have in stock a range of suitable papers and other materials that experience has shown will produce the best result. Its equipment will be sized to produce cost-efficient books, and its staff members will be able to assist you with all of the operations that go into the making of a book. They'll be able to show you samples of books of your type that they have printed. Their experience will really pay off when you are producing an unusual book, such as a children's book with pop-ups.

You will find book printers listed and classified by the types of book they do most in the "Printers" section of *Literary Market Place*. Once you locate some suitable printers, you can send them a manuscript and sample illustrations to get bids for printing your book.

When I first started publishing books via my own company Marsh Creek Press, we got bids from printers all over. The most reasonably priced printer turned out to be right here in our backyard, Book Printers of Utah, 1791 West 2300 South, Salt Lake City UT 84119; 801-972-5440 ph; 801-972-5441 fx. If we factored in shipping costs, they stood out even further. The reliability, quality, and timeliness of the printer count, too, not just the cost.

A colorful subject? Do it in color

We aren't limited to the old black and white anymore—color printing is easier to do now and less expensive. It isn't cheap, by any means, but less than a few years ago. I have a sign on my office wall that says

If it is necessary, the cost is irrelevant

That's not as silly as it might sound at first—the surgery, the strong dam, the trip to see someone who is seriously ill—all of these might cost you, but if necessary, the money is secondary. The same applies to the question of color in books. Books on interior decoration, guides to birds or wildflowers, or books with reproductions of color artwork for instance, can hardly do without color. It still will cost you, but if your book is good and delights the reader, it will pay off in the end. You know your subject and the audience it's intended for, and how critical color is (or isn't) to the purpose of your book.

Color is often confined to book covers alone, nothing inside, but if you are thinking about a colorful book, check it out before you rule it out. "Full color" comes from the four-color process—the combination of cyan (blue), magenta (red), yellow, and black (CMYK) layers of ink, from which all other colors are made. The reason color printing is expensive is that the preparation for it is complicated ("separations" and plates have to be made for every layer of color). Using color in a small run of books is costly—it will actually make you flinch—but for big runs, it averages out to a smaller cost per book. A color insert (say sixteen or thirty-two pages of color) can be done for less than color throughout the book. For one thing, the coated paper that color printing requires is more expensive than uncoated paper, so you save that paper cost in the rest of the book.

If your book has a lot of color illustrations, check out the printers who print overseas, such as in China, Korea, Singapore, and Japan. This is how the big publishers keep down color printing costs.

On very small printings, such as only a hundred or a few hundred copies, you can use the high-speed copiers that require no separations or plates. Thus the cost of color printing here can be little more than black and white, though the quality of reproduction will not be the same as printing done by the conventional printing process. Many local print shops have copiers of this type.

> In my office we often identify our books by the color of the cover. It's faster than using titles—we just say "the green book" (*Clutter's Last Stand)*, "the yellow book" (*Is There Life After Housework?),* or "the purple book" (*Don Aslett's Clean in a Minute).* Even my customers often remember and order them that way. Well, when we got to fifteen, we began to run out of colors! We now have a fluorescent-orange book and an aluminum-colored one, and may in desperation consider a leather-bound baby next. Writing is pretty exciting, and after many books it is only more so.

There is something called "two-color" printing, too, in which different colors of ink can be used, for either text or line illustrations. Used well for carefully chosen accents, this technique creates a colorful and attractive effect for much less money.

How many should you print?

When I self-published my first book, the much lower per-copy cost of a large print run was appealing, and as mentioned earlier it led me to order 20,000 copies for my first printing. I got lucky and sold them all fairly soon, but you can't count on that. Don't print too many in your first run. I'd do 1,000, 2,500, or maybe 5,000 if you have a bunch of seminars lined up. Even if you can afford to print them, you probably won't be able to store many more books than that.

As mentioned earlier, on-demand printing may be a way out of the book quantity bind. This method of printing is in effect high-quality photocopying. Before you sneer at that, bear in mind that regular offset printing (the method used to produce most books) is really only a superior form of photocopying. On-demand printers will produce any quantity of books (there may be a modest minimum, such as fifty copies) for the same unit price—50, 150, 1,500, or 15,000 books are all the same price per copy. You do need to supply them with the same thing you would supply a regular printer—the typeset, designed, and laid-out book on a computer disk. Some on-demand printers offer an editorial service for an additional fee that will design the cover and interior of your book for you. The bottom line here is that although the cost per copy will be higher than the cost per copy in a standard print run, you can end up with attractive, finished copies of your book without making a giant investment. If your book takes off and you need large quantities, you can use the printing materials you already have now to do conventional printing.

"Warehousing" your books

When my first big book order showed up at my house, man, was I unprepared. You don't store 20,000 books (hundreds of cases of them) in a bedroom closet. Our cars ended up being evicted from our two-car garage indefinitely.

So for your book, something you need to think about in advance is a safe, dry, and accessible place to put it. The printer will scream (and charge you!) if you try to leave your books with him while you figure out a good place to put them. Rental storage units will cost you $50–$150 a month—that adds up fast, and storing them away somewhere is an inconvenience. So right at home is a good place to do it.

There is very little chance that anyone will steal your books, even if you leave them outside on the street, so security isn't much of an issue, unless you're printing a color-illustrated guide to counterfeit cash. A dry, pest-proof place is what you need, and a spare bedroom, garage, or finished, dry basement is fine for the purpose. Just remember that books are heavy by the case. Carry four or five cases around, or up and down stairs, and you'll know it. So pick the most convenient storage place you can, and make sure it can take the weight!

Storing your books at home is handy and keeps you hard at work marketing them because you have to walk past them every day and would like to regain the space for its original purpose.

"It ain't heavy—it's my book."

Your book will mean more to you than a Mercedes or Lincoln, trust me, so the garage is in fact a good place for it.

Don't try to shoehorn all those books into someone else's house (your parents', children's or friends'). People don't like this, even if they claim it's okay. Keep them home with you.

Decide where you want to store your books, and be ready **before** the truck pulls in!

For any details of self-publishing you want to know more about, see the guides in the Resource List.

CHAPTER 11

To Market, to Market: Promoting and Selling Your Book

Now it's out, time to scout… and SELL, SELL, SELL?

No, the selling of your book, to family members, friends and acquaintances, business associates, fellow hobbyists/enthusiasts, or the world at large should have been done before and during the writing of it. If you wait until those precious volumes are bound and sitting out on the garage floor in forty or four hundred cases, you are getting a late start!

The time and place to start selling and marketing your book is the day you dream it up, before you even touch pen to paper. Right at the outset of your book project, make a folder of marketing ideas, and keep adding to it throughout the whole drafting and polishing process.

Most of us new writers have bookstore blindness—we tend to think that the bookstores are just panting to get our books and start selling them like hotcakes. This SELDOM HAPPENS. It's hard to sell books out of bookstores today because there are so many books and all kinds of big publishers who have been at it forever and have their feet in the door and ears to the market. So they can and do get their books onto the bookstore shelves and into airport racks and onto the big shows on TV. I've been in most of these places myself, and it can be done, but the big publishers can accomplish this much more easily and efficiently than you can right now. So don't sit around waiting for

Barnes & Noble to call you on the phone because someone heard about your marvelous new book.

You need to be a real hustler here—not a pitchman or movie star, just someone who turns over as many rocks as possible. Once you get started, you'll learn fast. Talking to other self-publishers and writers you'll learn all kinds of different ways they have found to sell their books. (And since they may be fibbing a little, cut the results they say they got in half, and that should give you a realistic view of things.)

Some sales outlets to consider

BOOKSTORES—Yes, you can approach them directly as a self-publisher. However, the big ones buy through wholesaler-distributors like Ingram and Baker & Taylor. The addresses of those companies can be found in the "Sales & Distribution" section of *Literary Market Place*. Bookstores are slow payers, and sometimes they don't pay.

DISTRIBUTORS, or SALES REPRESENTATIVES—There are many distributors (often called "independent reps" in the trade) who already sell books, calendars, and the like to bookstores and other stores. If your book fits the kind of subject matter they carry, they might be willing to add it to their "lines" or their catalogs. Lists of distributors and sales representatives can be found in *Literary Market Place* and *Jump Start Your Book Sales*, by Marilyn and Tom Ross, among other places.

BOOK CLUBS—They are always looking for good books. You have to discount your book here to almost nothing (how do you think they are able to make those fabulous "six books for $1" offers to new members?). But even a few cents per book on enough books adds up. And most publishers feel that book club sales don't cut into bookstore sales. Book clubs are also listed in *Literary Market Place*.

THE INTERNET—Amazon carries every one of my published books, and computer enthusiasts are always complimenting me for being on Amazon. Amazon wants big discounts, and unless your book is spectacular, having it offered here won't move all that many copies. But it will get your book out there for all the world to see. There are many other booksellers online, such as barnesandnoble.com, but none has the clout of Amazon.

You can also, of course, create your own website to sell your book. (See page 167 for more on selling via the 'net.)

"Today we needed some scrap paper in the office, so I brought in a box of printed promotional forms. We did these in 1995, and they cost us $500 for five hundred, of which about four hundred ended up wasted. Today we can do the same promotion to an email list for little or nothing, except the time to type it up.

The Internet as we know it today is still a Model T, but it won't be long before it becomes a Cadillac or Rolls. You can reach millions and millions of people, on not just a state or regional basis, but international, for your book on wallpapering or whatever. So if you need any incentive to explore web promotion and sales, bear in mind that every minute you put in today will be worth far more five years from now.

Find something on the web (a site) doing more or less the same thing you want to do, such as another writer self-publishing a book on model airplanes. Study what they did (how many pages the site has, what kind of illustrations, how many and what type of ads), copy it, and improve on it (as you would a magazine to the same audience you are designing a new magazine for). This is like a novice learning and playing the master, and then trying to improve on him."

—*ROHN ENGH, author,*
photographer, and photomarketer

"When my book *The Virgin Homeowner* came out, my publicist at the publisher left, leaving me with no publicity. So I set up my own war room and for thirteen months did all my own publicity. It kept the book alive, and when Oprah's producers were looking for a book for a show called "How Well Do You Know Your House?" they went to Amazon, and there it was with quite a number of glowing reviews. Long story short, I did the show three years after the book was published, and the show gave it a huge shot in the arm."

—*JANICE PAPOLOS,*
author and self-taught publicist

SEMINARS, WORKSHOPS, and SPEECHES—Another sales channel all authors should take advantage of (one reason you're writing, after all, is because you have a message everyone needs to hear). If you are a stirring speaker, a group of four hundred people may buy a hundred books and with an $8 profit per book, you've made $800 even if you give the speech for free. I've made thousands of dollars in minutes after a speech, with my children or grandchildren helping at a book sales table in the back of the room. Even when you speak to small groups, there will usually be a few book sales. And someone might be there who is interested in buying a copy of your book for every manager in her whole company, or whatever.

MAIL-ORDER—Get that book of yours in someone's mail-order catalog, and you can sell a respectable number, usually at retail price. Another way to approach mail-order sales is to find an organization that "fits" your book—be it a group of farmers, home schoolers, La Leche League members, motorcylers, or environmentally minded people. Make up an inexpensive brochure or exciting letter about your book (offering it at a "discount"), get a list of the membership, and send it to them. If one in fifty responds, you've got a new source of sales, and those single sources add up.

SALES OUT OF THE BACK OF THE BOOK—You can put an order blank in the back of the book, and if your book is good, readers will order more directly from you. I put a catalog page (see below) that includes all my books into every book I do.

PREMIUMS—Here is a real opportunity for a good book—bulk sales of part or all of it to companies like Rubbermaid, Nike, 3M, or your local savings and loan. The goal is to get a company or business to use your book for gifts, customer rewards or incentives, grand openings, conventions, and other special events. Unloading 5,000 or 20,000 books this way, even discounted 60–70 percent, means big bucks. I sold 5,000 copies of *Who Says It's a Woman's Job to Clean?* to a large furniture store for a grand-opening handout. I only made $.75 a book selling them a $6 book for $1.50, but it still added up to $3,750.

Be mindful of such possibilities as you write, and keep a list of them to suggest to your publisher or explore yourself when the book is finished, or even as you write.

SPECIALTY STORES—Is your book a natural to be sold in craft stores, sporting goods stores, or garden centers? Send the owners or managers of the store some books (say a dozen) to experiment with. Make them an offer they can't refuse. I've even left books on consignment in specialty stores to test the appeal to the market. You never know when the right person or place will come along.

LIBRARIES—These are great sales channels that every publisher has on its contact list, but self-publishers often miss out on. Find a library list, and approach it locally first. Good reviews of your book are one of the most powerful sales aids here.

Those are ten sales avenues, and there are at least two dozen more. See if you can find some on your own—be creative. Sales to TV shopping channels, selling door to door, at fairs or flea markets, to organizations, to fundraisers, to _____. The books in the Resource List will help here.

I sold all 20,000 of the first printing of my own first book in six months between seminars and the order blanks in the back of the book. I was a good marketer when I didn't know anything about marketing… maybe there is a message there. Just when you think there is no other way, something will appear if you keep tapping sources. A friend of mine with a book that was going nowhere got it featured on a can of beans, and it sold 200,000 copies by direct mail.

Doing more than one book has its advantages because all of your efforts in speaking and selling mean that later books can coattail off the first. You can also offer books together for a special discount price, such as three books at $10 each or all three for $19.95. So one sale will net you $16, even with a healthy discount.

The power of "in person"

During a meeting with a Sears executive once in Chicago, I learned a profound marketing principle called the "in-person demo." He showed me a Sears frypan and told me how many they sold with ads, coupons, and other print means. Then he showed me what happened when there was an actual human being showing and using the pan in front of a group. The difference wasn't just a little, it was astounding. One person in a hundred might buy after reading; with a demo one-third or more of the audience would buy.

The human presence conveys feelings of warmth and caring, especially these days when half of even phone calls end up with voice mail or answering machines. A stamped autograph on a book is almost a negative, worse than a blank title page. But when there is a real inscription on there from you, knowing that the author actually touched that book, people will treasure it. And then if you personally present or hand that book to someone, it puts it over the top.

The human touch is hard to come by today and can be a big factor in your book's sale. When people see and hear you expound the principles in your book and bring them to life, it becomes a bible. And then they will run out and tell twenty friends how great you and your book are because they actually met you!

With in-person sales, it's especially important to strike while the iron is hot. Jump right onto any positive response you get. People often buy now, and rarely "later." I did a big seminar in a small town in southern Utah once, for instance, and 350 enthusiastic, appreciative women bought cases of *Is There Life After Housework?* and *Do I Dust or Vacuum First?* They begged me for the new book about junk and clutter I'd said was on the press right now, *Clutter's Last Stand.* I could have taken eighty orders on the spot, but no, I told them I'd contact them as soon as the book was out.

When it was out, I ran a big ad in the local paper, including a special discount offer. When no response came, I called the paper and asked why it hadn't run the ad. The paper had run the ad and sent me a copy to prove it. Those fans were all out there somewhere, but I never sold a single book. So sell anything you have **now**, not later.

THE "HONOR SYSTEM" OF BOOK SALES (IT WORKS!)

I give many workshops and seminars around the country every year, and in the early days of this nearly my whole family came along to help handle the physical details and sell books. As the kids grew up and went on to responsibilities of their own, my wife and I and a helper from my office did the same as four or five of us did before. As time passed and I had to travel ever more and farther, and my wife became more involved in helping out the family and community, I was left alone to handle larger and larger crowds who still wanted to buy books. How was I able to do it?

Believe it or not, I sell more books with this system than when I had a person at the table, and in five years I haven't lost a book or a quarter. People respond well to being trusted.

On my book table I placed a little basket of money and a sign.

PUBLICITY

Publicizing your book begins with your announcement "I'm going to write a book," and will go uphill or downhill from there all depending on you.

Whether you self-publish or a publisher does it for you, the burden of publicity rests on your back. You are your book's parent and know more than anyone else in the world about it. So who better to carry the torch for it?

The bottom line is that no one will want or buy a book they know nothing about from an author they know nothing about. No matter how good your book, the word has to get out, and you have to be the willing trumpeter.

This means publicity. Publicity is what you see when you turn on your TV in the morning to see Katie Couric interviewing a veterinarian on the newest housebreaking techniques for puppies, and he just happens to be the author of a new book on the subject. Publicity is media attention. Publicity is generally free. Publicity gets the word out about your book to the public. Publicity triggers the thought, "I'm going to look for that book and buy it!"

To be invited for an interview—for TV, radio, or newspaper—you have to spark an interest in your topic in the TV or radio show producer or newspaper editor. One way is to send a press kit that contains your best pitch on you and your book, telling them why their audience would love to hear you talk about your area of expertise.

A press kit can be as simple as a pocket report folder with your book cover glued to the front. Inside you'll put a good photo of you, a photo of the book, some "wow" facts and ideas from your book, a press release about it, a brief biography of yourself, and any good press pieces about yourself you happen to have. Be sure to include a list of

On recent books we have gone to an e-media kit, such as the one below at www.donaslett.com for *Lose 200 Lbs. This Weekend.* This saves postage and makes the information instantly accessible to editors and producers around the world.

questions for the media to ask about your book and subject (so they don't even have to think up their own). You might even want to include a copy of the book itself, plus anything else that might help or get attention. For several of my books, we had great success with including a copy of a humorous self-test from the book—the "Junkee Entrance Exam" from *Clutter's Last Stand* and the "Are You a Macho Man?" quiz from *Who Says It's a Woman's Job to Clean?*

If your contact with them is compelling enough, any media person in his right mind will jump at the chance to interview you (or at least call when it's a slow news day).

A public figure—you?

Your next hurdle is the interview itself. Simply show up early, fully prepared with witty answers to the questions you gave them, plus any obvious others, and then watch the books move off the store shelf. The first few interviews are scary if you've never done TV or radio, but before long you'll do fine, and they'll never know this is your first book.

I've done more than 5,000 radio and TV interviews/segments, and they are still fun and productive. Just be ready and give them good stuff, and extra books to pass around. Then they will talk about you before you get to the studio, while you are there, and after you've gone home.

I, and many other authors, do the majority of radio and print interviews now by phone, and it's easy and inexpensive.

POINTERS ON RADIO AND TV

• Radio producers want you to be able to think fast and provide fast, punchy answers.

• TV producers are interested in "quick visual payoff," so be prepared to tell them what props you can bring and demos you can do.

• Newspaper reporters will appreciate any resources you have online—photos, illustrations, diagrams, articles—that they can download and reproduce in a flash.

• When you appear on radio or TV, it's in better taste and is more effective to let your host push your book instead of your constantly saying. "In my book I…." Before we go on the air or in front of the camera, I hand them a book and say, "Hey, man, you're the pro—you handle it, and I won't mention my book—you do it." They love this because then they don't have to worry about you pushing this too far.

• I keep records on all my interviews—where and when they were and what we talked about. You may hear from the same station or publication again, and it's good to know what you did and said the first time so you can keep track of what works well and not so well, and so you don't repeat yourself.

Promoting your own book via a website

The web is still a new and slightly awkward form at times, but it's here to stay. And a website is a handy and inexpensive way to let the world know about your book. So test and experiment, ask, look at what others are doing, and come up with something that works. Let's listen to a book writer whose experience gives some idea of the possibilities here:

"My book *The Bipolar Child* was marketed in two ways. Our publicist at Broadway Books was amazing and got us '20/20,' 'Oprah,' and NPR, among other important interviews.

I concentrated on 'seeding the 'net.' The book was due to be published in December, so in July of the summer before, my husband and I began to construct a website. We reserved all domains for www.bipolarchild.com/net/org and www.thebipolar-child.com/net/org so that no one else could use them. We began looking at sites in our field and saw some that we liked, so we contacted the webmaster. Once we went to work, it took about three months to create the site.

I don't think a website should merely sell a book. It needs to give out helpful information so that people **need** to visit it. I planned and incorporated a lot of useful content and committed to a bimonthly email newsletter to which people could subscribe.

Once we were live on the World Wide Web (three months prior to pub date), I began to contact other webmasters who had compatible sites in order to introduce them to our site and to inquire whether they would like to link to us.

I got on the search engines and punched in 'bipolar and

children,' and whenever I came across a site that seemed a good candidate for a link, I emailed the webmaster, introduced myself as the author (with my husband, Dmitri F. Papolos, M.D.) of our previous book, *Overcoming Depression,* and invited them to visit www.bipolarchild.com and possibly link to it. I pointed out that we had the first published IEP (Individual Education Plan) on that site and other very helpful information for parents and educators. Almost always I got a lovely note back from the webmasters with notification of arranged links (later I sent books to these people, and they reviewed the book online).

So, when the book was published, we already had several thousand copies reserved on Amazon. Knowledge of and demand for the book was there, and we came out of the starting gate at a fast clip.

Our email newsletter keeps the book cutting edge (serves as a sort of supplement), and people email it all over the world to friends, so it spreads the word about the book.

I want to remind authors that online chats are very important today in publicizing a book, so try to make those happen."

—*JANICE PAPOLOS,*
author and self-taught publicist

Reviews: effective, inexpensive promotion

Book reviews are one of the least expensive and most effective ways to promote your book. Marilyn Ross, coauthor of *The Complete Guide to Self-Publishing*, calls them "**the** foremost sales generator, after a sales force capable of selling sand to a sheik."

Especially for authors whose name is not yet a household word, reviews in publications like *Publishers Weekly* and *Library Journal* can make a big difference. The majority of libraries base their purchases on reviews in *Library Journal,* so a favorable review is very likely to land you a place on their shelves. And considering the number of books released every day, if *Publishers Weekly* picks up your book for review, that really helps with getting the books into both independent and chain bookstores. Sometimes, if a buyer at a national chain store is reluctant to take on a book, a favorable review in a trade magazine can help convince her to carry it.

The value of reviews does depend to some degree on the author and publisher. Books by John Grisham or Stephen King will probably sell regardless of reviews. And companies like Random House or Simon & Schuster publish so many books that if some don't get reviewed, it's not going to break them. However, for small publishers, it's critical to get as many reviews as they can.

If you're being published by a publisher, it should take care of sending books out for review. But if you know of specialized magazines or newsletters they might not be aware of, be sure to ask them to send review copies there, too. If you're self-publishing, don't forget to seek reviews (the books listed in the Resource List will tell you exactly how to go about this). You can even write your own reviews if necessary, and make good use of them!

Be especially mindful of the fact that some of the most important review media, including the ones mentioned above, must see books **while they are still in the proof stage** to consider them for review.

They read or you bleed! So your motto, when it comes to marketing your book, needs to be:

"I've got a message. It is in a new book. I can and will tell you about it—any time!"

CHAPTER 12

IT'S WORTH IT: THE REWARDS (AND A RECAP)

There are really only two big must-do's in writing a book

1. You've got to start somewhere.
2. You've got to end somewhere.

All of the talent, desire, imagination, and market potential in the world are worthless if you cannot or will not make these two steps in bookmaking. There are more good never-published authors in the world than successfully published authors simply because many people with the ability to really shine never start their book.

And millions of those who finally marshal the determination to start their books get lost somewhere along the way—half or three-quarters of the way into it they drift away or get discouraged. Some are 90 percent or more finished but keep worrying and working at it, twinking and dinging on it… forever, so their books die at the same exact minute they do.

It's a shame, when there are only two real rules for writing: You've got to start somewhere, and then you've got to wrap that baby up someday. You can only wait so long for that extra little piece the book needs. Never finishing finishes off many would-be authors!

The REWARDS of book writing

This is the real bottom line of your book, what it does for you. Often this is measured solely in terms of how much it makes when it comes to money. But if you spent two years of your spare time researching and writing and editing and illustrating and selling your book, and didn't make a lick of money, just broke even, or even used up your $5,000 of vacation money in the process, I'd wager you spent your time and money well. And benefited more—gained more personal satisfaction, wisdom, and popularity, more self-confidence, than any vacation could have given you. And definitely more than couch potatoing or chitchatting those two years away would ever have amounted to. Your book probably enhanced your professional status, as well.

A book writes you as you write it. It gives you dreams and hopes and puts good thoughts and noble ideas to work. It disciplines you, too—strengthens you and shores up weaknesses. And it does more to organize you than you can ever imagine.

I like how a book blesses my life by blessing others. I've had hundreds of phone calls and letters on how my books changed people's lives, brought marriages back together, stopped suicides, and changed whole families and businesses. Anything you do through your book to enhance the lives of others goes way beyond any profit and loss columns. I've seen average and even poor books take their authors into groups and lectures and trips, put sparkles in their eyes, speed up their pulses. Even if your book costs you, as long as it moves you and your readers to a new level of living and makes you a better writer, then you are a tremendously successful author.

Your book can also be a silent inspiration for your children or grandchildren to write. And one book will surely trigger another and even better one. They come faster and get easier with experience as you get your system smoothed out.

Again, I'll tell you from the heart of everything I've heard and seen and lived of the book business: If you are in it for the money alone, there are faster and better ways to make it. How many rich writers do you know? I know hardly any. But how many life-changing authors do you know? I know a lot.

How many rich writers do you know?
I know hardly any.
But how many life-changing authors do you know?
I know a lot.

To sum it all up now

Let me give you some summary charts now to help you keep your book project on track and ensure that it turns out a winner!

THE "GOOD BOOK" CHECKLIST
- ❏ A compelling subject
- ❏ A good title: clear, provocative, and as short as possible
- ❏ A good cover (you **can** tell a book by its cover)
- ❏ Provides a solution to the problem it poses
- ❏ Author who has credibility in the subject
- ❏ And is 100 percent committed to the book
- ❏ Attractive design and layout
- ❏ Well-organized, easy-to-use
- ❏ A style that makes you want to keep reading
- ❏ Lets the reader take part
- ❏ Art or photos that enhance the text
- ❏ The right size book for the subject
- ❏ Priced right
- ❏ Easy to find and buy on the bookshelf
- ❏ A table of contents and back cover that make anyone who picks the book up want to read it

---

THE STEPS TO BOOK SUCCESS

1. A good solid idea
2. A new angle on it
3. Good, satisfying information on the subject
4. A sound (well-organized) structure
5. An initial rough draft
6. A good edit
7. Finding, and filling in, the missing pieces
8. A revised and better manuscript
9. Good art and graphics
10. Marketing, marketing, marketing!

THE STEPS IN DOING A BOOK, IN BRIEF

Idea	➡	**Test market**	➡	**Adjust**
Commit	➡	**Outline**	➡	**Write**
Rewrite	➡	**Edit**	➡	**Rewrite**
Illustrate	➡	**Lay out**	➡	**Proof**
Print	➡	**Publicize**	➡	**Market**

Some final advice on your book:
• Don't flaunt it before you write it.
• Keep saving good "add on" material for revisions and updates of the book, or sequels.

WRITE TO ME

Do you have a question about writing and selling books that wasn't answered in these pages? Write to me and let me know what it is and I'll try to make sure it's answered in the next edition. Or you might just like to share your own experience writing and selling your first book.

Write to me at:
        Don Aslett
        PO Box 700
        Pocatello ID 83204

or email me at: aslettdon@aol.com

If you would like to be notified of the dates and locations of Don Aslett's "How to Write and Sell Your First Book" seminars, please send your name and address to the above.

BOOKS

Get Organized, Get Published! by Don Aslett and Carol Cartaino, Writer's Digest Books. How to get it all together and finally DO it (write that book, article, or story) and approach every part of the writing process in a more efficient and effective way.

Writer's Market. The classic guide to publishing companies, magazines, and agents and what they are looking for. Now available online (updated continually) and in print form (published annually), from Writer's Digest Books.

Writer's Guide to Book Editors, Publishers, and Literary Agents, by Jeff Herman, Prima Publishing. Editors, publishers, and agents identified, and their enthusiasms.

Directory of Small Press Magazine Editors & Publishers, Dustbooks.

Literary Market Place, or "LMP." The official directory to all aspects of the book business, published by R.R. Bowker.

Books in Print and *Forthcoming Books in Print,* R.R. Bowker. One of the best places to go to check out the competition for your book.

A Writer's Guide to Book Publishing, by Richard Balkin, Plume.

How to Get Happily Published: A Complete and Candid Guide, 5th edition, by Judith Appelbaum, HarperCollins.

How to Write a Book Proposal, revised edition, by Michael Larsen, Writer's Digest Books.

How to Write Irresistible Query Letters, by Lisa Collier Cool, Writer's Digest Books.

Kirsch's Guide to the Book Contract, by Jonathan Kirsch, Acrobat Books.

The Writer's Digest Guide to Manuscript Formats, by Dian Dincin Buchman and Seli Groves, Writer's Digest Books.

Guide to Literary Agents, Writer's Digest Books. Published annually.

How to Write & Sell Your First Novel, by Oscar Collier and Frances Spatz Leighton, Writer's Digest Books.

The Self-Publishing Manual: How to Write, Print and Sell Your Own Book, 13th edition, by Dan Poynter, Para Publishing.

Writing Nonfiction: Turning Thoughts into Books, by Dan Poynter, Para Publishing.

The Complete Guide to Self-Publishing, 4th edition, by Tom and Marilyn Ross, Writer's Digest Books. Everything you need to know to write, publish, promote, and sell your own book.

Small Publishers Association of North America Resource Directory of Independent Publishers and Publishing Industry Vendors, published by the Small Publishers Association of North America.

Publishers Weekly, published by Reed Business Information (this book industry magazine is online at http://publishersweekly.com).

The Chicago Manual of Style, 14th edition, University of Chicago Press (a complete guide to copyediting, indexing, and the elements of book production).

Chicago Guide to Preparing Electronic Manuscripts, University of Chicago Press.

Jump Start Your Book Sales: A Money-Making Guide for Authors, Independent Publishers and Small Presses, by Marilyn and Tom Ross, Communication Creativity.

Book Marketing: A New Approach: How to Sell Books to Bookstores, Libraries, and Nontraditional Markets, Para Publishing.

1001 Ways to Market Your Books, by John Kremer, Open Horizons Publishing Company.

Make Your Knowledge Sell: A Complete Guide to Selling Nonfiction on the Web, by Ken Evoy and Monique Harris, http://myks.sitesell.com.

BOOK SERVICE PROVIDERS
and INFORMATION CENTERS
for self-publishers and book writers

(See also the many references on pages 172–173 for others.)

Carol Cartaino
(freelance editor, book doctor, and book consultant)
2000 Flat Run Road, Seaman OH 45679
Phone: 937-764-1303
Email: cartaino@aol.com

Craig LaGory
(freelance artist and designer)
6413 Roe Street, Cincinnati OH 45227
Phone: 513-271-4818

About Books, Inc.
(help with all and any stages of your book, and the marketing afterward)
PO Box 1500, 425 Cedar Street, Buena Vista CO 81211-1500
Phone: 719-395-2459
Fax: 719-395-8374
Email: marilyn@about-books.com
Website: www.about-books.com

Jenkins Group, Inc.
(help with all and any stages of your book, and the marketing afterward)
400 West Front Street, #4A, Traverse City MI 49684
Phone: 800-706-4636
Fax: 231-933-0448
Website: www. bookpublishing.com
Magazine: *Independent Publisher*

Dan Poynter/Para Publishing
(help with all and any stages of your book, and the marketing afterward)
PO Box 8206, Santa Barbara CA 93118-8206
Phone: 805-966-7277
Fax: 805-968-1379
Website: www.Parapub.com

GLOSSARY

Like every country and profession, we book people have our own culture and vocabulary. Once into the world of books, you'll hear many new terms and expressions. Here is the equivalent of that little dictionary you buy when you're visiting a foreign country and need to say please, thank you, or "where is the bathroom?"

AA's, or author's alterations Changes made by the author when reviewing proof (when all those last-minute doubts and improvements suddenly come to mind). If you change more than ten percent of the type, most publishers will charge you for it.

ABI (Advance Book Information) This is a form you fill out to make sure your book is included in *Books in Print* and *Forthcoming Books in Print*, the volumes that let everyone in the book industry and elsewhere know that your book exists or is coming.

acknowledgments A page or two in front of the book, or sometimes in back, where you thank everyone who helped bring your book into being.

acquisitions editor An editor who spends most of his or her time finding new books for the company to publish and convincing their authors to sign with *this* publisher.

adaptation A special edition of a book done for some special purpose, and usually changed a bit for the purpose.

advance Money the publisher agrees to advance you against your book's eventual earnings. Advances are usually paid in two or more installments, such as when the book contract is signed and when you deliver an acceptable manuscript.

appendix, appendices Material that is good reference or background material for your subject, but too dull, technical, or detailed to stick right into the text proper. So it's put in the back of the book.

auction When a literary agent or author gets a number of publishers excited about a book and bidding against each other for it. (Every author's dream!)

autograph The author's actual signature on a book, usually on the title or half-title page.

backlist Book publishers usually release their new books and do a catalog twice a year, in spring and fall. The backlist is all of the older books (published before the current season) a publisher carries that it is still selling.

back matter Material that appears at the back of the book after the text proper. Backmatter includes things like the epilogue, appendices, and index.

bad break When a word, headline, or page is broken in an awkward and unattractive way during typesetting.

bestseller A very loose term—it can mean anything from books listed on one of the established bestseller lists, such that compiled by the *New York Times*, to simply "books currently selling very strongly."

bibliography As used in trade books, this means a list of the books and other sources consulted when writing a book.

bleed A printing term for ink going clear to the edge of a page. "Four-sided bleed" is ink bleeding off all four sides of the page. Part of the specifications to determine cost of printing.

blues or blueprints The very last stage of proofs you see, right before a book goes to press. They're called blues because they actually are blue, and made from the film the book will be printed from. Any changes here better be really worth making because corrections in the blues stage are expensive. Many printers now offer direct-to-plate printing, which eliminates the need for film and blues. Printers provide digital proofs instead, and changes are both cheaper and easier to make.

blurb A strong selling statement (usually no more than a sentence or two) that appears on the cover or jacket of a book near the title—the "killer" copy that is supposed to push you over the edge to buying it.

BookExpo America (formerly ABA, after the American Booksellers Association) The yearly exhibit, held in a huge exposition center, of the wares of all of the publishers in the U.S., thousands of booths full of books. The book industry's convention.

book "doctor" An editor who helps manuscripts with serious problems, or that need a lot of work, get where they need to be.

book packager Companies who specialize in thinking up ideas for books and then selling them to publishers. The packager's staff then writes, illustrates, and produces the book for the publisher for an agreed-upon price per copy.

book printer A printer who specializes in producing books.

book rate A special, lower postage rate that the Post Office lets you use for books, videos, and other educational materials. This is used to be called "special fourth class rate," and is now called "media mail." It isn't speedy, but it's cheaper.

caption A line of type accompanying an illustration or photograph, identifying or describing it.

CIP data Cataloging-in-Publication information supplied by the Library of Congress for the copyright page of a book telling librarians where and how to catalog it in a library.

coated stock Paper coated with clay or other materials to make it slick and smooth. Coated stock is often used for books containing illustrations, particularly photographs.

collaborator A partner or partners you take on to co-write your book with you. Collaborators, as opposed to ghostwriters, usually get title page and cover credit.

colophon Several lines of type somewhere in the front matter of a book (often on the copyright page) that tell you who edited the book, designed it, illustrated it, oversaw the production of it, and sometimes even what paper and typefaces were used and where it was printed.

color insert Color illustrations added by gluing or sewing a group of pages (usually sixteen or thirty-two) between the signatures of the book proper.

color separations Negatives made in preparation for color printing that translate all of the colors of the original into the limited number of colors of ink (usually four) actually used to print.

commercial rights The rights to make dolls or keychains or whatever based on your book (nonbook products based on it, or characters in it).

content editing Editing that concerns itself primarily with larger issues, such as is the book doing what it's supposed to do, covering what it's supposed to cover, is it in the right order, and is it satisfying in general.

copyediting "Nit-picking editing" that combs over the whole manuscript to make sure spelling, grammar, and punctuation, are all correct, smooths out your sentences where necessary, and calls to your attention any oversights, contradictions, or overlooked small matters of content.

copyright The official, legal ownership of an artistic work you have produced, such as a book.

crop, cropping Removing part of a photograph or illustration to heighten its impact or help it fit.

cross-reference Note within a book that refers you to somewhere else in the book, such as See page 53.

custom book producer One of the growing number of companies that offer a whole range of services to a self-publisher: everything from helping you write, or improve and perfect the manuscript, to designing it, illustrating it, laying it out, and printing it for you. They may also offer help with marketing and publicity.

dedication A statement in the front matter, usually fairly brief, of whom you dedicate all of your hard work on this volume to.

delete The word writers hate—the one that means "take this out, remove it, cut it."

design, book: The choices and decisions (as to typefaces, spacing, headlines, use and placement of illustrations, and the like) that give your book its overall appearance, or "look."

developmental editing Another term for content editing. Guidance and feedback the editor provides as the manuscript is written to help keep the author on track.

direct mail Selling books directly to the customer by mail.

disclaimer Wording put in the front matter of your book to help prevent legal problems or injury claims from readers. See page 151 for an example.

draft A manuscript in not-yet-final form.

dramatic rights The rights to make your book into a movie, play, TV series, or other dramatic form.

ebook A book that can be downloaded onto your computer from the Internet. A book on screen, not paper.

editorial director Another term for editor-in-chief. Often an editorial director oversees a group of imprints or editorial departments.

editor-in-chief The head editor of a publishing house or an imprint within it.

endorsements Praises or recommendations of your book by other people, preferably well-known and important ones.

endpapers The stiff pages at the very front and back of a hardcover book used to glue the book to its binding. Endpapers are sometimes decorated.

epilogue A minichapter or short piece at the very end of a book that sums it up, makes a revelation, or tells what happened later.

fair use The amount of text it is generally assumed you can quote from other published sources without having to get permission, as long as you say where it came from and do not quote it in some damaging way. Most publishers feel that quoting 250 words from a book-length work or 100 words from an article or short story is safe. (This refers to prose, not poetry or song lyrics, whose publishers are more paranoid.)

first edition The very first form your book comes out in before it is revised or put in a different kind of binding.

first serial Running of some part of a book in a periodical, such as newspaper or magazine, usually before the book itself is published.

flap copy The copy on the "flaps" of a book jacket that hold it on, meant to impress you with the author and seduce you into reading the book.

font Another word for typeface. A complete set of letters, numbers, and punction marks for a given type size and design.

footnote A note in the bottom margin of a page, usually in smaller type, that explains something about, or gives a reference for, something mentioned in the text.

foreword A piece in the front of the book by someone other than the author praising it or describing its scope.

Frankfurt Book Fair The mega book exposition in Frankfurt, Germany, where book publishers from around the world come to wheel and deal and show their wares.

frontispiece An illustration facing the title page.

front matter Material that appears in the front of a book, such as title page, copyright page, dedication, and table of contents.

ghostwriter Someone who writes something under someone else's name, getting no byline credit or public recognition for it.

glossary A little "dictionary" included in a book defining terms used in it, or in the subject matter it covers.

gutter (of a book) The white space between two facing pages—the margins that extend from the inner edge of the text of those pages, toward the binding.

half-title An optional page in the front of a book that comes before the title page and repeats at least part of the title.

imprint, publisher's A different name that a publisher may put on some of its lines of books. Goose Publications, for example, may also have the imprints Greylag Press and Aunt Rhody, Inc. The books published within an imprint often have their own distinctive character.

index A section in the back of a book that, if properly done, gives the page numbers of anything you might want or need to locate in the book.

in-stock date When a book has been printed and shipped to bookstores, when it is in stock, available.

introduction A piece by the author that appears before chapter one, introducing the subject matter and explaining the scope and intent of the book, etc.

ISBN International Standard Book Number—a number printed on the copyright page and back cover of a book that unmistakably identifies it among the millions of other books out there. Each edition of a book (paperback, hardcover, revised, etc.) will have its own ISBN.

jacket or "dust jacket" The paper cover put over the binding of a hardcover book, with a hopefully attention-getting design and the title, author's name and photo, and sales copy of all kinds on it.

libel Writing that injures the reputation of a person or company, causing them to look bad and lose money.

line drawing A drawing that is black and white, without shading, tones of gray, or screening.

line editing Editing that focuses, line by line, on smaller issues such as the smoothness and clarity of individual sentences.

list All the books a publisher has in print.

list price The official retail price of a book, the full, undiscounted price.

literary agent Person who agrees, for a commission, to attempt to sell authors' books to publishers. If he succeeds, he will then attempt to negotiate the most favorable terms possible and act as the author's advocate during the whole life of the book.

LMP (*Literary Market Place*) The official directory of the book industry, published by R.R. Bowker.

lowercase non-capital letters, such as this.

managing editor The person at a book publisher who oversees and coordinates the flow of manuscripts from the editorial department (where developmental and content editing are done) to the production department, where the copyediting is done and the book will be physically produced.

manuscript A book in its original (usually typed) form, before it is typeset, laid out, or printed.

mass-market paperback The small paperback books you see in racks at the airport and drugstore. They are cheaper to produce than trade paperbacks and are sold through an entirely different distribution system than trade books and often published by different publishers.

net receipts (or "publisher's net receipts") The amount a publisher actually receives for a sale of books or the rights to them, minus any discounts, commissions, or the like.

on-demand publishing A form of printing that produces books in small quantities or even single volumes, if and when they are actually needed.

option The contractural right to publish an author's next book, or to at least have the first chance to review and consider it.

out of print A book that is no longer being produced or sold by its publisher, or carried in its catalog.

out of stock The publisher has run out of copies of the book and is in the process of reprinting it.

overkill My term for "too much" of anything.

page proofs Proofs of the book after it has been typeset and laid out into pages.

part-title See half-title.

perfect binding A glued binding for paperbacks that results in a book with a square back.

permissions Written permission from the copyright holders to include material from copyrighted sources in your book.

plagiarize Copying what someone else has done too closely, such as word for word (we all adopt ideas and angles from others).

point-of-purchase display A special display rack or box to sell a book in a highly visible place, such as on the counter.

pre-publication price A special lower price offered to buyers if they will agree to buy a book before it is published.

preface A short piece by the author in the front of the book before the beginning of the book proper. Technically, the distinction between this and an introduction is that the preface often includes an explanation of why you did the book the way you did, other books you owe a debt to, etc.

press kit A packet of promotional material sent to the media or anyone to get attention for your and your book.

proofer's marks The little symbols proofreaders, printers, and other book production people use to mark corrections on proofs or layouts. You can find a list of these in the *Chicago Manual of Style*.

proofreader A person who reads the typeset pages or other parts of a book to catch any errors the typesetter or printer may have made.

proposal A detailed description of a book drawn up before it is written, composed in such as a way as to try to convince a publisher to give you a contract to write that book.

pseudonym A fake name or "pen name" an author uses instead of his own when he does not wish his identity to be known.

publication date The official date on which a finished book is launched into the world. Publishers usually make this a date weeks or even months after the book has rolled off the press, to give time for prepublication publicity.

Publishers Weekly, **or "PW"** The best-known magazine of the book industry.

query A letter written to a book publisher or magazine, asking if it might be interested in your book or article idea. Queries should be as provocative and compelling as possible

rejection You send your book or book idea to a publisher, but it turns down the project.

remainders Books the publisher has left over, an overstock of, or despairs of ever selling. Remainders are sold to discount booksellers at a low price, and you may have the right by contract to buy them.

reprint As used in the book business, an additional printing after the first.

repro The final version of the typeset, laid-out, and corrected book, ready to be made into printing plates.

reserve against returns The portion of your royalty earnings that a book publisher does not pay you but holds in reserve in case the books that appear to be sold all come sailing back. The amount a publisher is allowed to hold as a reserve against returns is stipulated in the contract.

returns Books a bookstore can't sell, or can't sell quickly, that are sent back to the publisher for refund.

review copy Books sent to newspapers, magazines, and other possible reviewers in hopes that they will read it and write a review.

review Commentary on, or an evaluation of your book by a newspaper, magazine, or other "review medium."

revision A reissue of a book, with changes, corrections, and usually additions. To qualify as a revision, a book must technically be changed at least 20 percent.

royalties The term for the money the author makes from a book— usually some percentage of the retail or wholesale price.

running head The little line of type at the top of the page that tells you (on the left-hand page) the title of the book, and on the facing page, the name of the chapter you are in now.

sans serif Type without the tiny "feet" a serif typeface has everywhere the letters touch the dotted lines that would be there if those words were being drawn in a penmanship book. Sans serif type is clean and modern-looking, but hard to read in large quantities. This is a sans serif typeface.

second serial Publication of part of your book somewhere (usually in a magazine) after the book itself has been published.

self-cover A hard cover with no jacket, but a jacketlike design printed right on the cover and usually laminated.

self-publishing Doing everything necessary to publish and market a book yourself, rather than having a publisher do it.

short run Though the definition of this term may vary a bit, in general it means a book printing of 3,000 copies or less.

signature Books are printed in large sheets, and one entire sheet, when folded up into pages, makes a signature—usually a group of sixteen or thirty-two pages. A number of signatures are then bound together to make the complete book, and this is why the total page count of books is usually some multiple of sixteen or thirty-two.

slipcase A cardboard case enclosing one or more books.

slush pile That huge pile of unsolicited and unread manuscripts in an overworked editor's office. The place you want to stay out of.

softcover Another word for paperback.

spine The "back" of a book, the part you see when books are put onto a shelf in the usual way.

style sheet The sheet a copyeditor keeps all through his work on a book, recording the ways in which words, numbers, and all of the other concerns of a copyeditor have been styled, of the options available (e.g., is that color going to be spelled gray or grey?)

subsidiary rights The rights to do anything else you can do with a book besides publish it in the regular edition—anything from mass-market paperback rights to pamphlet rights to the right to make an audiotape, computer game, movie, or toy series out of it.

subsidy press A publisher that will publish your book if you pay it a healthy "stipend" (fee) to help them do so.

subtitle A secondary title many books have (the part after the colon, if there is one), usually to help clarify or explain what the book is about.

table of contents The page or pages in front of a book that list the chapters and where they can be found. A "TOC" may also include a brief description of each chapter, called an annotation.

tip in A separate page, or group of pages, glued into a book between the signatures, such as a full-color stain-removal chart added to a black-and-white book on cleaning.

title page The first page of a book, with the title and subtitle of the book, author's and illustrator's names, and the publisher's name.

trade books Books written and published for the general public, the kinds of books sold in bookstores, as opposed to, for example, textbooks.

trade or quality paperback The larger, full-size paperbacks (as opposed to smaller or rack size paperbacks) sold in bookstores.

trim size The dimensions of a finished book. This term comes from the fact that book pages are printed a little larger than the actual page size, and then trimmed by knives to produce a clean edge.

two-color printing Printing in two different colors of ink so that you can have, say, the text in one color and line illustrations in another.

typesetting Getting the words of a book manuscript from the original form it was typed in, into a form suitable for the printer to reproduce from. This is a much simpler process today in the computer age than not long ago when it meant going from typewritten manuscript to type set by a printer.

university press A press affiliated with a college or university that usually does books of a more scholarly nature. Many university presses do regional books and some trade books, as well.

uppercase Capital letters. Using all capital letters, LIKE THIS, is called full caps.

vanity press A company that agrees to produce a book for you for a certain sum of money. Vanity publishers often advertise aggressively for customers and may create the impression they are actually publishing your book. In general, vanity publishing is less respected than self-publishing.

wholesaler, book Companies, such as Baker & Taylor, that buy books for resale to bookstores and libraries.

widow A very short line or single word on a line in some awkward and very visible spot in a book layout.

working title The initial title you give your book while you are working on it.

INDEX

Don's secrets to success as an author:

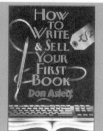

HOME MANAGEMENT: **GET MORE DONE:**

VIDEOS:

TITLE	Retail	Qty	Amt
Clean in a Minute	$5.00		
Video Clean in a Minute	$12.95		
Cleaning Up for a Living	$16.99		
Clutter Free! Finally & Forever	$12.99		
Clutter's Last Stand	$12.99		
Construction Cleanup	$19.95		
Don Aslett's Stainbuster's Bible	$11.95		
Everything I Needed to Know…Barnyard	$9.95		
For Packrats Only	$13.99		
GET ORGANIZED, GET PUBLISHED!	$18.99		
How to Be #1 With Your Boss	$9.99		
How to Handle 1,000 Things at Once	$12.99		
How to Have a 48-Hour Day	$12.99		
How Successful People... Out of the Toilet	$14.95		
How to Upgrade & Motivate Your Crew	$19.95		
How to Write & Sell Your First Book	$18.99		
Is There Life After Housework?	$11.99		
Video Is There Life After Housework?	$19.95		
Keeping Work Simple	$9.95		
LOSE 200 LBS. THIS WEEKEND	$12.99		
Make Your House Do the Housework	$14.99		
NO TIME TO CLEAN!	$12.99		
Painting Without Fainting	$9.99		
Pet Clean-Up Made Easy	$12.99		
Professional Cleaner's Clip Art	$19.95		
Video Restroom Sanitation Includes Quiz Booklet	$69.95		
Speak Up	$12.99		
The Cleaning Encyclopedia	$16.95		
The Office Clutter Cure	$10.99		
The Pro. Cleaner's Handbook	$10.00		
Who Says It's A Woman's Job…	$5.95		
Wood Floor Care	$9.95		
500 Terrific Ideas for Cleaning Everything	$5.99		

Shipping: $3 for first book or video plus 75¢ for each additional.	Subtotal	
	Idaho res. add 5% Sales Tax	
	Shipping	
	TOTAL	

☐ Check enclosed ☐ Visa ☐ MasterCard ☐ Discover ☐ American Express

Card No. _____

Exp Date _____ Phone _____

Signature X _____

Ship to:
Your Name _____

Street Address _____

City ST Zip _____

V&S 05/0219

MAIL your order to:
Don Aslett **OR Call**: 888-748-3535
PO Box 700 **Fax**: 208-235-5481
Pocatello ID 83204

☐ Don, please put my name and the enclosed list of friends of mine on your mailing list for the *Clean Report* bulletin and catalog.

Other Aslett books you won't want to miss...

EASY CLEANING:

NEW—DECLUTTERING:

MORE ON CLEANING:

BUSINESS & MISC:

  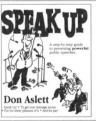   

FOR PROFESSIONAL CLEANERS:

Don's secrets to success as an author:

HOME MANAGEMENT: **GET MORE DONE:**

VIDEOS:

TITLE	Retail	Qty	Amt
Clean in a Minute	$5.00		
Video Clean in a Minute	$12.95		
Cleaning Up for a Living	$16.99		
Clutter Free! Finally & Forever	$12.99		
Clutter's Last Stand	$12.99		
Construction Cleanup	$19.95		
Don Aslett's Stainbuster's Bible	$11.95		
Everything I Needed to Know...Barnyard	$9.95		
For Packrats Only	$13.99		
GET ORGANIZED, GET PUBLISHED!	$18.99		
How to Be #1 With Your Boss	$9.99		
How to Handle 1,000 Things at Once	$12.99		
How to Have a 48-Hour Day	$12.99		
How Successful People... Out of the Toilet	$14.95		
How to Upgrade & Motivate Your Crew	$19.95		
How to Write & Sell Your First Book	$18.99		
Is There Life After Housework?	$11.99		
Video Is There Life After Housework?	$19.95		
Keeping Work Simple	$9.95		
LOSE 200 LBS. THIS WEEKEND	$12.99		
Make Your House Do the Housework	$14.99		
NO TIME TO CLEAN!	$12.99		
Painting Without Fainting	$9.99		
Pet Clean-Up Made Easy	$12.99		
Professional Cleaner's Clip Art	$19.95		
Video Restroom Sanitation Includes Quiz Booklet	$69.95		
Speak Up	$12.99		
The Cleaning Encyclopedia	$16.95		
The Office Clutter Cure	$10.99		
The Pro. Cleaner's Handbook	$10.00		
Who Says It's A Woman's Job...	$5.95		
Wood Floor Care	$9.95		
500 Terrific Ideas for Cleaning Everything	$5.99		

Shipping: $3 for first book or video plus 75¢ for each additional.	Subtotal	
	Idaho res. add 5% Sales Tax	
	Shipping	
	TOTAL	

☐ Check enclosed   ☐ Visa   ☐ MasterCard   ☐ Discover   ☐ American Express

Card No. _____

Exp Date _____ Phone _____

Signature X _____

Ship to:
Your Name _____

Street Address _____

City ST Zip _____

W&S 05/0219

MAIL your order to:
Don Aslett   **OR Call**: 888-748-3535
PO Box 700   **Fax**: 208-235-5481
Pocatello ID 83204

☐ Don, please put my name and the enclosed list of friends of mine on your mailing list for the *Clean Report* bulletin and catalog.

Other Aslett books you won't want to miss...

EASY CLEANING:

    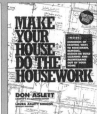

NEW—DECLUTTERING:

MORE ON CLEANING:

BUSINESS & MISC:

FOR PROFESSIONAL CLEANERS:

 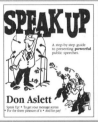   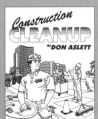

200